OPHULS

Edited by **Paul Willemen**

1978

Published by/British Film Institute/127 Charing Cross Road, London WC2H 0EA

Acknowledgments

Cover still: *Lola Montes* (courtesy of Artificial Eye).

I would like to thank the following people and organisations for their generous assistance: Jon Halliday, Deirdre McCloskey, the National Film Archive (Jeremy Boulton), David Meeker, Artificial Eye (Andi Engel), Barrie Ellis-Jones for his translations from German, Robin Mann for the translation of *The Pleasure of Seeing, Wide Angle* (Peter Lehman) for permission to reprint *The Question Oshima,* Carl Hanser Verlag (Christoph Schlotterer), Frieda Grafe and Enno Patalas for permission to reprint sections from the book *Im Off,* the *Deutsche Zeitung/Christ und Welt* (B Inhoff) for permission to reprint *The Pleasure of Seeing,* Marcel Wall-Ophuls, *Cahiers du Cinema,* Alan L. Williams, Angela Martin, Jennifer Batchelor, the staff of the BFI-Publications Dept.

This book has been produced to accompany a season at the Edinburgh Film Festival and a (nearly) complete retrospective organised by the BFI's Film Availability Services, presented by the NFT and FAS at the National Film Theatre, London.

ISBN 0 85170 0829

Contents

Preface

Towards the end of his essay in this book, Stephen Heath formulates what I regard as *the* pertinent question to be asked of all books on the work of directors (or reviews of individual films, for that matter):

"Is an interest in 'the work of Max Ophuls' today anything more than academic, the province of film studies and criticism? The question perhaps of the Edinburgh retrospective? That 'Ophuls' is the name of a certain exasperation of the standard Hollywood production of his time is no doubt the case, as it is too that that exasperation is a veritable mannerism of vision, and of vision of the woman — with the masquerade become the very surface of the text, laid out, *exposed:* the masquerade of 'the woman' (the luxurious feminine of jewellery, furs, mirrors . . .), THE masquerade of 'the woman in film', cinema's object, pursuit-and-goal (the ceaseless enunciation of the ceaseless fascination of the ceaseless tracking of the woman for the gaze, the look, of appropriation which, in its extreme in *Madame de . . .*, is near itself to the impossibility known, half-seen)."

However, the formulation of a reply, that is to say, an account of the discursive/institutional determinants, which, hierarchically organised, combine to produce the present booklet — is 'impossible' from a position within the institution. 'Impossible' because the institutional organisation of discourses is such that there is no 'subject position' available within it from which an enunciation of an analysis of that institution as a regime of discourses and practices can be spoken.

Paul Willemen

Familmographic Romance

Paul Willemen

The following notes include, besides the usual filmographic data, some indications of the various discourses (political, erotico-familial, economic, etc.) which run through and to some extent help locate all or part of the work that is generally ascribed to Ophuls and which forms the object of this book. The information has been drawn from remarks by Claude Beylie, Richard Roud, Max Ophuls, Hilde Wall-Ophuls, Marcel Wall-Ophuls, George Annenkov and a few other sources. However, it is clear that the 'Ophuls' reconstructed by, e.g., Claude Beylie has little in common with the one produced by Annenkov, or that the 'husband' is different from the 'father'. Indeed, the 'Ophuls' constructed by Max Ophuls in his memoirs and interviews is in many ways — and how could it be otherwise — a phantasy figure, a fictional character. Moreover, all these informants, in conveying their constructions, adhere to the rules of one of the most rigorously coded journalistic genres: the artist's life story. As such, the 'biographic' information constitutes no more than the remnants of an outline for the construction of what Freud called a family romance: the melodrama of the life of the 'great' artist. Except that, in this instance, most of the obvious melodramatic features so insistently present in, e.g., Claude Beylie and G. Annenkov's books on Ophuls have been omitted, offering the possibility of a new narrative, another romance. The information included here concentrates on the signposting of certain sets of discourses in which 'Ophuls' was/is embedded and which produced him as a specific character in the dramatic narrative called 'film history'. Obviously, people speaking from a particular ideological position (or better, through whom certain idealist ideological discourses speak) will endeavour to unify the disparate sets of discourses referred to by positing Ophuls as the place where these discourses find their coherence. And, to some extent, this chronology invites such an activity. However, it does so only to the extent that the 'object' of the book has been prefabricated by film-distribution and exhibition practices as well as by critical discourses and historical narratives: the acquisition of 'Ophuls' films for distribution, the organisation of 'Ophuls' retrospectives, this publication entitled 'Max Ophuls' in a way legitimising and reproducing the unity of the object 'Ophuls'. What the neologistic title of this chapter then seeks to convey, is precisely an invitation to read this 'bio-filmography' against the grain, against the industrial and ideological, institutional pressures which dictate that 'Ophuls' shall be a unified object of study and that there shall be a relation of identity between the character produced through remarks of informants and the biological individual who ceased existing in 1957.

Finally, the romance also includes selected bibliographic information, limited to the main articles written by Ophuls and a signposting of the places where and the ways in which Ophuls has been taken up, constructed as a ‘classic’ and inserted in critical and institutional discourses. In other words, the charting of the consacration of a ‘great artist’ and the way such a trajectory is affected by critical/theoretical discussion.

In conclusion, a note on Ophuls’ name: although written with an umlaut in German, Ophuls insisted, later, that the sign of germanicness be erased, e.g. from the credits of his post-war French films. Secondly, the American version of his name, Opuls, never caught on. So throughout this book, the director is referred to as Ophuls, without an umlaut and with the ‘h’.

1902 Born Max Oppenheimer in Saarbrücken, an industrial town in the Rhine valley. His family had been successful in the textile industry and belonged to the well-off bourgeoisie. Ophuls’ mother came from a firmly established bourgeois family of the area.

The Saar is a rich coalmining country, with Saarbrücken located almost on the border with France. From 1919 to 1935, the Saar was occupied by the French under the banner of the League of Nations. Following a plebiscite in 1935, it was restored to Germany. From 1945 to January 1, 1957, the French again occupied the area, and although they didn’t plunder its natural resources as openly and viciously as they had done before, at the 1957 plebiscite the Saar once more elected to return to Germany.

Ophuls’ mother tongue was German and that is the language in which he wrote. Although he spoke French fluently from an early age, he never lost his definitely German accent. French was a most important cultural and political presence in his formation as a film maker, given that it also symbolised the rejection of the Third Reich.

1914 World War I, followed by prolonged French occupation of the Saar.

1919 In an effort to avoid becoming the second term in a company that might be called Oppenheimer & Son, Max wrote some drama journalism for local papers (four drama reviews signed M.O. appeared in the *Saarbrücken Zeitung* in 1920, but whether they are definitely by Ophuls remains an open question), toyed with the idea of becoming a circus or variety performer, and then decided to embark on a career as a stage actor. In order not to shame the family name, he adopted the pseudonym Ophuls. Apparently, the name was chosen by his mentor, the stage director Fritz Holl, in memory of a young Danish actress with whom Holl, once upon a time, was supposed to have been hopelessly in love. Moreover, one of the reasons why Holl agreed to become Ophuls’ mentor in spite of Max’s decidedly limited talents as an actor, was, again according to Ophuls, that Holl was also supposed to have been in love with Max’s mother. Ophuls alleges he became an actor because they appeared to lead glamorous sex lives with women waiting at the stage door every evening.

1923 After a few years as an extra with walk-on parts in repertory companies, performing all kinds of plays and operas in a wide variety of styles, Ophuls was given the opportunity to direct a play in Dortmund. His account of the event is that he was hired as a dramatic and a comic actor, but after seeing him in a comedy the manager threatened to cut his salary in half, retaining only the dramatic part. The only way to keep his full salary was to accept to double-up as director as well. He took the offer and has remained a director ever since, limiting his desire to perform as an actor to the acting out of his instructions, and to the giving of lectures.

1923-5 Successful career as a director, first in Dortmund where he staged about 200 plays, and at Elberfeld-Barmen where he directed operettas. Simultaneously, to supplement his income ('In Cologne, Stuttgart, Frankfurt, Elberfeld, everywhere I worked, living beyond my means . . .') he worked for radio, first as literary reviewer, then adapting plays and stories, reading poetry, directing musical shows, sketches and radio plays. He was to continue this radio work throughout his life, developing a format that could be described as a 'literary show': a mixture of extracts from novels, poetry etc ranging across a wide variety of styles, combined with improvisational pieces, reflections and comments, parodies and so on, the whole interwoven with sound and music effects.

1926 Spent a few months in Vienna directing at the prestigious Burgtheater. In Vienna, he met and married Hilde Wall, a well-known dramatic actress at the time, who abandoned her career after her marriage.

1927 Directed and/or supervised about thirty plays in Frankfurt, where he functioned first as musical director and then as Oberregisseur (director-in-chief) at the New Theatre. The plays he staged included works by Stefan Zweig, Büchner, Schnitzler, Zuckmayer and Gogol as well as Edouart Bourdet, Israel Zangwill, Ferdinand Raimund and Jacques Natanson. Birth of his son, Marcel Wall-Ophuls.

1928-9 Worked as director at the municipal theatre in Breslau, where he staged plays by Shakespeare, Molière, Kleist, Shaw, Pagnol, Ben Hecht and A.-P. Antoine's *L'Ennemie* (later filmed by M.O. as *La Tendre Ennemie*). Wrote and directed a children's Christmas play dedicated to his son, about two boys in the belly of a whale: *Fips und Stips auf der Weltreise* (published by Drei Marken Verlag, Berlin 1929, 43 pages, roneo MS). The music was by Hans Krieg. According to Marcel Ophuls, the play wasn't performed very often, while according to Max it was translated into various languages and performed throughout middle-Europe. The first performance was at the Lobe Theatre in Breslau on December 16, 1928.

1929 Wrote the marching song *Murmeln (Murmuring)* sung by Ernst Busch. Apparently this song had some success and was taken up in the Soviet Union. It was re-published in Germany after the war.

1930 A radical theatre group invited Ophuls to Berlin to direct one of their plays at the Lessing Theatre. He subsequently directed Ferber and Kaufmann's comedy *The Royal Family* at the Barnowski Theatre in Berlin. He continued writing songs and revue material including the song *Langeweile (Boredom)* with music by Harry Ralton and interpreted by Rudolf Platte. Contributed an article on avant-garde theatre to the magazine *Die Szene,* Vol. 20, No. 211. Worked as assistant translator on Anatol Litvak's *Nie Wieder Liebe,* shot simultaneously in German and in French. The French version, entitled *Calais-Douvres,* was directed by Jean Boyer.

As a famous theatre director who had shown an interest in the cinema and who apparently could handle dialogue, Ophuls was invited by UFA to make a comedy featurette.

DANN SCHON LIEBER LEBERTRAN (Rather Cod Liver Oil)
Directed by Max Ophuls; Prod. Co.: UFA (Berlin); Sc: Emeric Pressburger and M.O., adapted from Erich Kästner's story; Ph.: E. Schufftan. *Cast:* Käthe Haack (*mother*), Paul Kemp (*St Michael*), Heinz Günsdorf (*St Peter*), Hannelore Schroth (*daughter*). Running Time: 40 mins (other sources give 25/30 mins)

1931 Directed one important play at the Barnowski Theatre, made one film (see below), spent two months preparing a comedy film with Heinz Rühmann before abandoning the project and started shooting *The Bartered Bride.*

DIE VERLIEBTE FIRMA (The Company in Love).
Directed by Max Ophuls; Prod. Co.: D.L.S. (Berlin); Sc.: Hubert Marischka and Fritz Zeckendorf adapted by M.O. and Bruno Granischtädten; Ph.: Karl Puth; Music: Bruno Granischtädten, with Grete Walter and Ernst Hauke. *Cast:* Gustav Fröhlich, Anny Ahlers, Hubert von Meyerinck, Leonard Steckel, Ernst Verebes, Werner Finck, Lien Deyers, Jose Wedorn, Fritz Steiner, Hermann Krehan. Running time: 73 mins. Released in 1932.

1932 DIE VERKAUFTE BRAUT (The Bartered Bride).
Directed by Max Ophuls; Prod. Co.: Reichsliga Film (Munich); Sc.: M.O., Curt Alexander and Jaroslav Kvapil, adapted from Smetana's comic opera *Prodana nevesta;* Ph.: Reimar Kuntze, Franz Koch, Herbert Illig, Otto Wirsching; Music arranged by Theo Mackeben. *Cast:* Willy Domgraf-Fassbaender (*Hans),* Karl Valentin (*Circus director*), Liesl Karlstadt (*his wife*), Anita Sörensen (*Esmeralda*), Mad Nadler (*Mayor Krusinova*), Jarmila Novotna (*Marie, his daughter*), Paul Kemp (*Wenzel*), Otto Wernicke (*impressario*), Max Schreck, Hans Appel, Therese Giese (*woman at photography booth*), Georg Holl, Lotte Deyers, Lothar Körner, et al. Running time: 77 mins.

LACHENDE ERBEN (Merry Heirs)
Directed by Max Ophuls; Prod. Co.: UFA (Berlin); Sc.: Trude Herka from her own story, adapted by M.O. and Felix Joachimson; Ph.: Eduard Hoesch; Music: Clemens Schmalstich and Hans Otto Borgmann. *Cast:* Heinz Rühmann, Lien Deyers, Lizzi Waldmüller, Max Adalbert, Ida Wüst, Julius Falkenstein, Walter Jannsen, Friedrich Ettel. Running time: 76 mins.

LIEBELEI
Directed by Max Ophuls; Prod. Co.: Elite Tonfilm (Berlin); Prod.: Fred Lissa; Sc.: Curt Alexander, Hans Wilhelm and M.O., based on the play by Arthur Schnitzler; Ph.: Franz Planer; Music: Brahms, Mozart, Beethoven,

arranged by Theo Mackeben. *Cast:* Wolfgang Liebeneiner (*Lt Fritz Lobheimer*), Magda Schneider (*Christine Weiring*), Luise Ullrich (*Mizzi Schlager*), Willy Eichberger [Carl Esmond] (*Theo Kaiser*); Gustaf Gründgens (*Baron Eggersdorff*), Paul Hörbiger (*Hans Weiring*), Olga Tschechova (*Baroness Eggersdorff*), Werner Finck (*musician*), Theo Lingen (*theatre director*), Lotte Spira, Walter Steinbeck, Bruno Kastner. Running time: 88 mins. Banned after WW II by Allied Military Governments.

Ophuls also staged two theatre plays, including H. Bahr's *Der Star,* starring Germany's most prominent actress of the time Käthe Dorsch.

1933 The day after the Reichstag fire, Ophuls and his family left Germany for Paris, where he quickly finished a French version of *Liebelei,* entitled *Une Histoire d'Amour.* Only the close-ups and some of the interiors were re-shot with Ted Pahle on camera, the rest of the film was dubbed. Apparently, the Third Reich censors removed Ophuls' name from the credits of the very successful *Liebelei.*

1934 Worked on *Le Scandale,* based on the play by Henri Bataille, but he was replaced as director by Marcel L'Herbier.

ON A VOLÉ UN HOMME (A Man has been Stolen)
Directed by Max Ophuls; Prod. Co.: Fox Films Europe (Paris); Prod.: Eric Pommer; Sc.: René Pujol; Ph.: René Guissart; Music: Bronislaw Kaper and Walter Jurman. *Cast:* Henri Garat (*Jean de Lafay*), Lili Damita (*Annette*), Fernand Fabre (*Robert*), Charles Fallot (*Victor*), Nina Myral (*old lady*), Pierre Labry (*man with scar*), Robert Goupil (*Legros*), Raoul Marco, Guy Repp, et al. Running time: 90 mins.

LA SIGNORA DI TUTTI (Everybody's Lady)
Directed by Max Ophuls; Prod. Co.: Novella Films (Milan); Prod.: Emilio Rizzoli; Sc.: Curt Alexander, Hans Wilhelm and M.O. based on the novel by Salvator Gotta; Ph.: Ubaldo Arata; Music: Daniele Amfiteatrof. *Cast:* Isa Miranda (*Gaby Doriot*), Nelly Corradi (*Anna*), Memo Benassi (*Leonardo Nanni*), Tatiana Pavlova (*Alma Nanni*), Federico Benfer (*Roberto*), Andrea Cecchi, Lamberto Picasso, Attilio Ortolani, Alfredo Martinelli, Giulia Puccini, Luigi Barberi, et al. Running time: 97 mins.

1935 In a plebiscite, the Saar province voted for reunification with Germany. Ophuls voted for integration into France.

DIVINE
Directed by Max Ophuls; Proc. Co.: Eden Prods (Paris); Prod.: Paul Bentata; Sc.: Collette from her book *L'Envers du Music Hall,* adapted by J. G. Auriol and M.O.; Ph.: Roger Hubert; Music: Albert Wolff; Songs by Roger Feral and J. G. Auriol; Ed.: Leonide Moguy. *Cast:* Simone Berriau (*Ludivine Jarisse-Divine*), Catherine Fonteney (*her mother*), Yvette Lebon (*Roberte*), Georges Rigaud (*Antonin*), Marcel Vallée (*director*), Gina Manès (*Dora*), Philippe Heriat (*Lutuf-Allah*), Sylvette Fillacier (*Gitanette*),

Thérèse Dorny (*'Poison'*), Paul Azaîs (*Victor*), Gabriello (*Nero*), Nane Germon (*Zaza*), Jeanne Véniat (*Mme Martelli*), Pierre Juvenet (*guard*), Jeanne Fusier-Gir (*Mme Nicou*), Roger Gaillard (*Pierre-Paul*), et al. Running time: 80 mins.

1936 The music critic Emile Vuillermoz set up a production company in Lyon called Compagnie des Grands Artistes Internationaux, dedicated to the promotion of musical 'culture', i.e. the 'classics'. He commissioned a series of short films entitled *Cinéphonies,* two of which were directed by Ophuls.

VALSE BRILLANTE DE CHOPIN
Directed by Max Ophuls; Prod. Co.: CGAI for Fox Films; Ph.: Franz Planer. *Cast:* Alexandre Brailovski (*piano player*). Running time: 6 mins.

AVE MARIA DE SCHUBERT
Directed by Max Ophuls; Prod. Co.: CGAI for Fox Films; Ph.: Franz Planer. *Cast:* Elizabeth Schumann (*singer*). Running time: 5 mins.

LA TENDRE ENNEMIE
Directed by Max Ophuls; Prod. Co.: Eden (Paris); Sc.: A.-P. Antoine, Curt Alexander and M.O. based on the play by Antoine *L'Ennemie;* Ph,.: Eugen Schufftan; Music: Albert Wolff. *Cast:* Simone Berriau (*Annette Dupont*), Catherine Fonteney (*her mother*), Georges Vitray (*her husband*), Marc Valbel (*her lover, Rodrigo*), Jacqueline Daix (*her daughter*), Maurice Devienne (*her fiancé*), Lucien Nat (*sailor*), Pierre Finlay (*Uncle Emile*), Germaine Reuver (*Aunt Jette*), Laura Diana (*girl at Maxim's*), Camille Bert (*Dr Desmoulins*), Roger Legris, Liliane Lesaffre, et al. Running time: 69 mins.

This film was released late in the year, after *Komedie om Geld.* Ophuls was invited to the Soviet Union and offered a two year contract. He returned from Moscow after two months. In Moscow, he published an article in *Das Wort* (the paper of the German left-wing refugees published in Moscow) praising Gustav von Wangenheim's anti-Nazi film *Kämpfer,* reprinted in *Filmkritik* in *1977*).

KOMEDIE OM GELD (The Trouble with Money)
Directed by Max Ophuls; Prod. Co.: Cinetone (Amsterdam); Sc.: Max Ophuls, Walter Schlee, Alex de Haas; Ph.: Eugen Schufftan; Music: Max Tak; Music arranged by Heinz Lachmann. *Cast:* Herman Bouber (*Brand*), Rini Otte (*Willy*); Mattieu van Eysden (*Ferdinand*), Cor Ruys (*director Moorman*). Running time: 81 mins. A bastardised version was released in Holland in 1953.

1937 Some abortive projects include a comedy by Yves Mirande, eventually made by Mirande and Georges Lacombe, and a film about Maria

Tarnowska, a famous Russian *femme fatale* at the centre of a crime of passion in 1919.

YOSHIWARA
Directed by Max Ophuls; Prod. Co.: Milo Films (Paris); Prod.: M. Milakowski, Sc.: Maurice Dekbora, based on his novel, adapted by Arnold Lipp [Lippschutz], Wolfgang Wilhelm, Jacques Companeez; Ph.: Eugen Schufftan; Music: Paul Dessau. *Cast:* Pierre-Richard Willm (*Lt Serge Polenoff*), Michiko Tanaka (*Kohana*), Sessue Hayakawa (*Isamo*), Foun-Sen (*Kohana's sister*), Roland Toutain (*Pavlik*), Camille Bert (*commander*), Lucienne Lemarchand (*Namo*), Gabriello (*Mr Po*), Leon Larive (*sailor*), Ky Duyen, Georges Paulais, et al. Running time: 90 mins.

1938 Ophuls obtained French nationality.

WERTHER
Directed by Max Ophuls; Prod. Co.: Nero Films (Paris); Prod.: Seymour Nebenzahl; Sc.: Hans Wilhelm and M.O. based on J. W. Goethe's novel; Dialogues: Fernand Crommelynck; Ph.: Eugen Schufftan; Music: Paul Dessau's arrangements of Schubert, Haydn, Mozart, Beethoven and Grétry; Script girl: Jacqueline Audry. *Cast:* Pierre-Richard Willm (*Werther*), Annie Vernay (*Charlotte*), Jean Périer (*the president*), Jean Galland (*Albert Hochstätter*), Paulette Pax (*Aunt Emma*), Georges Vitray (*bailiff*), Roger Legris (*servant*), Jean Buquet (*Charlotte's brother*), Génia Vaury (*prostitute*), Denise Kerny (*servant*), et al. Running time: 85 mins.

1939 SANS LENDEMAIN
Directed by Max Ophuls; Prod. Co.: Gray Film (Paris); Prod.: Gregor Rabinovitsch; Sc.: Jean Villème [Hans Wilhelm], Jean Jacot [Hans Jacobi], André-Paul Antoine and M.O.; Ph.: Eugen Schufftan; Music: Allan Gray. *Cast:* Edwige Feuillère (*Evelyn Morin*), Georges Rigaud (*Dr Georges Brandon*), Daniel Lecourtois (*Armand*), Paul Azaîs (*Henri*), Gabriello (*Mario*), Georges Lannes (*Paul Mazuraud*), Michel François (*Pierre*), Jeanne Marken (*Mme Bèchu*), Mady Berry (*Evelyne's concierge*), Pauline Carton (*Ernestine*), et al. Running time: 82 mins.

Ophuls complained that he had never seen a complete version of this film.

1940 DE MAYERLING À SARAJEVO
Directed by Max Ophuls; Prod. Co.: B.U.P. Française (Eugène Tuscherer); Prod.; Ivan Foxwell; Sc.: Curt Alexander, M.O., Marcelle Maurette, Jacques Natanson and A.-P. Antoine based on the story by Carl Zuckmayer; Ph.: Curt Courant and Otto Heller under the supervision of Eugen Schufftan; Music: Oscar Strauss; Ass. Directors: Jean Faurez and Jean-Paul Dreyfus [Le Chanois]. *Cast:* Edwige Feuillère (*Countess Sophie*), John Lodge (*Archduke Franz Ferdinand*), Aimé Clariond (*Prince Montenuevo*), Jeam Worms (*Emperor Franz Joseph*), Gabrielle Dorziat

(*Archduchess Maria Theresa*), Aimos (*Janatchek*), Jean-Paul Dreyfus [Le Chanois] (*Prinzip, the assassin*), Jean Debucourt (*Minister of Foreign Affairs*), Marcel André (*Archduke Friedrich*), Collette Régis (*Archduchess Isabella*), Henri Bosc, Jacques Clariond, Francine Claudel, et al. Running time: 89 mins. U.K. title: *Sarajevo.*

Ophuls was called up in 1939 before he had finished the *Mayerling* film, but towards the end of the year he was granted leave in order to complete it, although he had to manage with a reduced crew. He also had to abandon a project for a propaganda film about the Foreign Legion after shooting just one scene, as the many extras were ordered to the front. He participated in some anti-Nazi radio propaganda and eventually, together with his family, joined the exodus from Paris, fleeing to Aix-en-Provence, then to Marseilles. The theatre group of Louis Jouvet, sponsored by the Vichy Government, helped the family Ophuls across the border into Switzerland. In Zurich, Ophuls started a film of the Jouvet Company's performance of Molière's *L'Ecole des Femmes.* Only the opening sequence-shot had been completed when the producer pulled out. In Zurich also, Ophuls directed two plays, *Romeo and Juliet* and Ch. Feiler's comedy *Henry VIII and his Sixth Wife.* Although successful, Ophuls was unable to obtain a work permit in Switzerland unless he declared himself to be a deserter from the French army, which he refused to do. He had to re-cross into France to arrange passage to the USA.

1941 Arrived in Hollywood, where he experienced a long spell of unemployment, constantly punctuated by promises of work and invitations to select scripts for possible films.

1945-6 Wrote his autobiography; later published under the title *Spiel Im Dasein,* which can be translated in a number of ways combining the terms 'Play' (as in 'theatre play', as the substantive or as the imperative of the verb) and 'existence' or 'being-there'.

1946 Preston Sturges invited Ophuls to direct *Vendetta* for Howard Hughes and RKO to launch the career of Faith Domergue. But after a few days he was taken off the film as a result of severe disagreements with Sturges who represented the interests of Hughes. Subsequently, the film was directed by Sturges, Stuart Heisler, Hughes himself and it was finally released as directed by Mel Ferrer.

1947 On the suggestion of Robert Siodmak, Douglas Fairbanks Jr asked Ophuls to direct *The Exile,* which was finished and released the next year.

1948 THE EXILE

Directed by Max Ophuls; Prod. Co.: Fairbanks Co. Inc. for Universal International; Prod.: Douglas Fairbanks Jr; Sc.: D. Fairbanks Jr, based on Cosmo Hamilton's novel *His Majesty The King;* Ph.: Frank [Franz] Planer; Music: Frank Skinner. *Cast:* Douglas Fairbanks Jr (*Charles Stuart*), Maria Montez (*Countess of Courteuil*), Paule Croset (*Katie*), Henry Daniell (*Col. Ingram*), Nigel Bruce (*Sir Edward Hyde*), Robert Coote (*Pinner*), Otto Waldis (*Jan*), Eldon Gorst (*Seymour*), Colin H. Wright (*Millbank*), Colin Kenny (*Ross*), Peter Shaw (*Higson*), Will Stanton (*Tucket*), et al. Running time: 95 mins; originally tinted in sepia.

LETTER FROM AN UNKNOWN WOMAN
Directed by Max Ophuls; Prod. Co.: Rampart Prods for Universal; Prod.: John Houseman; Sc.: Howard Koch from a story by Stefan Zweig; Ph.: Franz Planer; Music: Daniele Amfiteatrof. *Cast:* Joan Fontaine (*Lisa Berndle*), Louis Jourdan (*Stefan Brand*), Mady Christians (*Frau Berndle*), Marcel Journet (*Johann Stauffer*), Art Smith (*John*), Howard Freeman (*Herr Kastner*), John Good (*Lt Leopold von Kaltnegger*), Leo P. Pessin (*Stefan Jr*), Otto Waldis (*concierge*), Erskine Sanford (*porter*), Sonia Bryden (*Frau Spitzer*), Carol Yorke (*Marie*). Running time: 90 mins.

Released in cut versions only (3 mins cut in the USA, 4 mins in Britain), the film was not shown in Britain until 1950, and then only in outer London and in the provinces. As a result of the intervention of the *Sequence*-critics (Gavin Lambert and Karel Reisz) a run in central London was arranged six months after the British première. The *Sequence*-critics (including Lindsay Anderson) were to continue their interest in Ophuls even when they were writing for *Sight and Sound,* laying the foundations for that magazine's interest in the 'fifties, leading to Richard Roud's index of Ophuls' work published in 1958 and the retrospectives at the National Film Theatre.

1949 CAUGHT
Directed by Max Ophuls; Prod. Co.: Enterprise Studios for MGM; Prod.: Wolfgang Reinhardt; Sc.: Arthur Larurents from the novel *Wild Calendar* by Libbie Block; Ph.: Lee Garmes; Music: Frederick Hollander; Editor: Robert Parrish; Ass. Director: John Berry. *Cast:* Barbara Bel Geddes (*Leonora*), Robert Ryan (*Smith Ohlrig*), James Mason (*Larry Quinada*), Frank Ferguson (*Dr Hoffmann*), Curt Bois (*Franzi*), Marcia Mae Jones (*Leonora's sister*), Ruth Brady (*Maxine*), Natalie Schaefer (*Dorothy Dale*), Art Smith (*psychiatrist*), et al. Running time: 88 mins.

THE RECKLESS MOMENT
Directed by Max Ophuls; Prod. Co.: Walter Wanger for Columbia; Prod.: Walter Wanger; Sc.: Henry Garson and R. W. Soderberg, adapted by Mel Dinelli and Robert E. Kent from E. S. Holding's *The Blank Wall* in the Ladies' Home Journal; Ph.: Burnett Guffey; Music: Hans Salter; Ass. Director: Earl Bellamy; Sets: Frank Tuttle and Cary Odell. *Cast:* James Mason (*Martin Donelly*), Joan Bennett (*Lucia Harper*), Geraldine Brooks (*Beatrice Harper*), Henry O'Neill (*Mr Harper*), David Blair (*David Harper*), Roy Roberts (*Nagel*), Francis Williams (*Sybil*), Shepperd

Strudwick (*Ted Darby*). Running time: 82 mins.

Throughout his career in Hollywood, Ophuls' name had been changed to Opuls.

Walter Wanger set up a project in Paris, a film of Balzac's *La Duchesse de Langeais,* to be directed by Ophuls. But soon after Ophuls' arrival in Paris, the project fell through for lack of money. Ophuls stayed on in Paris.

1950 In July, *Sight and Sound* published a short interview with Ophuls.

LA RONDE
Directed by Max Ophuls; Prod. Co.: Sacha Gordine; Sc.: Jacques Natanson and M.O. from the play *Reigen* by Arthur Schnitzler; Ph.: Christian Matras; Music: Oscar Straus. *Cast:* Anton Walbrook (*narrator),* Simone Signoret (*Léocadie, the prostitute*), Serge Reggiani (*Franz*), Simone Simon (*Marie*), Jean Clarieux (*brigadier*), Daniel Gélin (*Alfred*), Robert Vattier (*Prof. Schüller*), Danielle Darrieux (*Emma Breitkopf*), Fernand Gravey (*Charles*), Odette Joyeux (*young woman*), Marcel Mérovée (*Toni*), Jean-Louis Barrault (*Robert Külenkampf*), Isa Miranda (*Charlotte*), Charles Vissière (*concierge*), Gérard Philipe (*Count*), Jean Ozenne, Jean Landier, René Marjac, Jacques Vertan. Running time: 97 mins.

1952 LE PLAISIR
Directed by Max Ophuls; Prod. Co.: Stera Films CCFC (Paris), F. Harispuru and Ben Barkay; Sc.: Jacques Natanson and M.O. based on three stories by Guy de Maupassant, *Le Masque, La Maison Tellier* and *Le Modèle;* Ph.: Christian Matras and, for *Le Modèle,* Philippe Agostini; Music: Joe Hajos and Maurice Yvain with themes from Offenbach. *Cast:* (Ist episode) Claude Dauphin (*doctor*), Janine Viénot (*his friend*), Jean Galland (*Ambroise, the masked man*), Gaby Morlay (*Denise, his wife*), Paul Azaïs (*the director of the dance hall*), Emile Genevois (*the bellboy*), Gaby Bruyère (*Frimousse*), Huguette Montréal, Liliane Yvernault (*dancers*), (2nd episode) Madeleine Renaud (*Mme Tellier*), Danielle Darrieux (*Rosa*), Jean Gabin (*Joseph Rivet*), Ginette Leclerc (*Flora*), Paulette Dubost (*Fernande*), Mila Parély (*Raphaële*), Mathilde Casadesus (*Louise*), Amédée (*waiter*), Michel Vadet (*sailor*), Jo Dest (*the German*), Claire Olivier (*Mme Tourneveau*), Georges Vitray (*the captain*), Arthur Devère (*employee*), Charles Vissière (*old man from Normandy*), Zélie Yzelle (*his wife*), Pierre Brasseur (*Julien Ledentu, salesman*), Helena Manson (*Marie Rivet*), Joëlle Jany (*Constance Rivet*), René Blancard (*mayor*), René Hell, et al.; (3rd episode) Daniel Gélin (*Jean*), Simone Simon (*Joséphine*), Michel Vadet (*journalist*), Jean Servais (*narrator*), René Pascal, Marcel Reuzé. Running time: 95 mins.

A fourth sketch for *Le Plaisir,* to be called *La Femme de Paul* was abandoned for lack of money.

Ophuls also insisted that the umlaut on the 'u' in his name be scratched from the credit sequence of *Le Plaisir*. Abandoned projects included:

Autumn from an original script by Ophuls and Peter Ustinov, and *Love of Four Colonels,* based on Ustinov's play. *Sequence* published an analysis of Ophuls' work by Karel Reisz. Lecture by Ophuls at the British Film Institute-Summer School in Edinburgh.

1953 MADAME DE . . .

Directed by Max Ophuls; Prod. Co.: Franco-London Films (Paris) and Indusfilms/Rizzoli (Rome); Sc.: Marcel Achard, Annette Wademant and M.O. based on the novel by Louise de Vilmorin; Ph.: Christian Matras; Music: Georges Van Parys, Meyerbeer and Oscar Strauss. *Cast:* Danielle Darrieux (*Countess Louise de . . .*), Charles Boyer (*General André de . . .*), Vittorio De Sica (*Baron Fabrizio Donati*), Mireille Perrey (*nanny*), Jean Debucourt (*Rémy, jeweller*), Serge Lecointe (*Jerôme*), Jean Galland (*Mr de Bernac*), Hubert Noël (*Henri de Maleville*), Madeleine Barbulée (*a friend of Mme de . . .*), Jean Degrave (*debtor*), Georges Vitray (*journalist*), Beauvais (*butler*), Léon Walther (*manager of the theatre*), Guy Favières (*Julien*), Jean Toulout (*Ambassador*), Robert Moor (*diplomat*), Claire Duhamel, Germain Stainval, Emile Genevois, Pauléon, Collette Régis, Paul Azaîs, Albert-Michel, Georges Paulais, Michel Salina, René Worms, et al. Running time: 100 mins.

Published the essays; *Dichter und Film (Poet and Film)* in the magazine *Theater und Zeit,* Vol. 1, No. 2; *Einfall und Kontrolle (Inspiration and Control)* in *Filmforum,* vol. 2, No. 10. Projects included a film based on Nancy Mitford's *The Blessing,* to be produced by Alexander Korda, later directed by Sidney Franklin; and a version of *Mam'zelle Nitouche* with Fernandel, which fell through because of disagreements with the producer, Robert Hakim. The film was later made by Yves Allegret.

Ben Eichsfelder [Enno Patalas] published an article on Ophuls in *Filmforum,* Vol. 3, No. 3.

1954 In Baden-Baden, Ophuls directed for radio an adaptation of Goethe's *Novella,* released on record in 1959 in the series *Cottas Hörspielbühne.* Apparently, at this time Ophuls approached the ORTF (French TV) with a project for a series of biographical films based on H. W. Van Loon's *Lives.* One of the directors of the ORTF programming sections, Mr. Jean D'Arcy, is reputed to have suggested that he might perhaps find this 'young man' seeking a career in TV a job as an apprentice somewhere in the organisation.

Ophuls published: a piece on censorship in *Cahiers du Cinéma* No. 42; the essay *Die Lust Am Sehen (The Pleasure of Seeing)* in the *Deutsche Zeitung* (reprinted in this booklet) and *Kunst Findet Immer Wege (Art always finds a way).*

1955 LOLA MONTES

Directed by Max Ophuls; Proc. Co.: Gamma Films/Florida Films (Paris), Unionfilms (Munich)-Albert Caraco; Sc.: Jacques Natanson, Annette Wademant, M.O. (and Franz Geiger for the German version) based on the novel by Cecil Saint-Laurent *La Vie Extraordinaire de Lola Montes;* Ph.: Christian Matras – Cinemascope and Eastmancolour; Music: Georges Auric; Ass. Directors: Willy Picard, Tony Aboyantz, Claude Pinoteau, Marcel Wall [Ophuls]. *Cast:* Martine Carol (*Maria Dolores Porriz Y Montes, Countess of Lansfeld*), Peter Ustinov (*circus director*), Anton Walbrook (*Ludwig II*), Ivan Desny (*Lt James*), Lise Delamare (*Mrs Craigie*), Henri Guisol (*Maurice*), Paulette Dubost (*Joséphine*), Oscar Werner (*student*), Will Quadflieg (*Franz Liszt*), Jacques Fayet (*steward*), Daniel Mendaille (*captain*), Jean Galland (*baron's secretary*), Claude Pinoteau (*Claudio Pirotto*), Willy Eichberger [Carl Esmond] (*doctor*), Werner Finck (*painter*), Helena Manson (*James' sister*),et al. Running time: 140 mins (cut to 110 mins for release).

A second version, drastically re-edited, was released under the same title in 1957 which ran 90 mins with a special epilogue and a commentary-voice off spoken by Martine Carol. U.K. title: *The Fall of Lola Montez.*

Ophuls published *Hollywood Little Island* in *Cahiers du Cinéma,* nr 54; wrote articles for the *Darmstädter Echo* (27.3.55), *Die Filmwoche* (29.6.55), *Die Welt* (20.8.55). Truffaut wrote on Ophuls for *Art*, June 55; Enno Patalas and Henri Agel wrote on M.O. in *Antares,* vol.3, Nos. 2 and 3 respectively.

1956 Directed, in Baden-Baden, the radio version of *Frau Bertha Garlan* based on Schnitzler's story. Published a tribute to the broadcasting executive Friedrich Bischoff in *Linien eines Lebens;* held a lecture in Hamburg, later published as *My Experience;* published *Ein Kapitel Uber den Film und Seine Leute (A Chapter on Film and its People)* in *Deutsche Zeitung und Wirtschaftszeitung,* Vol. II, No. 26; *Gedanken über den Film (Thoughts on Film),* a lecture performed in Frankfurt and later transformed into a radio play (reprinted in this book); articles in the *Deutsche Zeitung* (31.3.56), *Frankfurter Neue Presse* (2.6.56), *Weser Kurier* (17.11.56) and *Der Kurier-Berlin* (15.9.56 and 22.11.56).

Cahiers du Cinema published two reviews of *Lola Montes* in their January issue (No. 55) together with an essay on Ophuls, and a few issues later (No. 59), a translation of Ophuls' essay *Der Letzte Drehtag (The Last Day of Shooting).*

A series of prominent critics and artists published an open letter defending *Lola Montes* and praising Ophuls as an avant-garde artist.

Film project: *Modigliani,* later directed by Jacques Becker as *Montparnasse 19.*

Eugene Archer published *Max Ophuls and the Romantic Tradition* in Yale French Studies.

1957 Directed *Der Tolle Tag,* i.e. Beaumarchais' *Marriage de Figaro,* at the Schauspiel Theater in Hamburg. He was hospitalised the morning of the premiere and died three months later, on March 26, in Hamburg. He was buried at the Père-Lachaise cemetery in Paris. Publication of *Regisseur aus unglücklicher Liebe (Director because of unrequited love)* in *Bonner Rundschau* (27.3.57); *Gertreide bleibt immer, aber der Film? (Grain is* *here to stay, but film?)* in *Der Bote* (30.3.57). *Cahiers du Cinéma,* nr 72, published an interview with Ophuls by Truffaut and Rivette (re-printed in this booklet), while *Cinema 57* also published a special issue (No. 18). *Sight and Sound* published a series of anecdotes as a tribute to Ophuls. Truffaut again published a tribute in *Arts* (April), entitled *Notre Cinéaste de Chevet (Our Bedside Cineast). Bianco e Nero* printed a filmography, while Pierre Leprohon devoted a chapter to Ophuls in his book *Présences Contemporaines* (Paris).

1958 Claude Beylie published *Max Ophuls*, Club du Livre de Cinema, Brussels.

Cahiers du Cinéma published another Ophuls-issue, No. 81, containing articles by Ophuls, translations of the anecdotes from *Sight and Sound* and notes on the Ophuls-retrospective at the Cinémathèque Française. Richard Roud: *Max Ophuls-An Index* (British Film Institute, London).

1959 Henri Agel devoted a chapter to Ophuls in his book entitled *Les Grands Cinéastes* (Paris); publication of Ophuls' memoirs, *Spiel Im Dasein* (Stuttgart), later serialised in *Cahiers du Cinéma* (Nos. 117 sqq.).

1960 University thesis on Ophuls by Gerard Syr at the I.D.H.E.C. (unpublished). Jacques Demy's *Lola* was released, containing a tribute to *Lola Montes* and the work of Ophuls.

1962 Georges Annenkov, *Max Ophuls,* Le Terrain Vague, Paris. The Swiss magazine *Cinema* published a special issue on Ophuls.

1963 Publication of the French translation of Ophuls' memoirs in book form: *Max Ophuls par Max Ophuls* (Eds Robert Laffont, Paris). Claude Beylie: *Max Ophuls,* in the series *Cinéma d'aujourd hui,* No. 16 (Seghers, Paris).

Script of *La Ronde* published in the series *L'Avant Scène du Cinéma.* National Film Theatre, London, organised its first Ophuls retrospective.

1964 Re-publication of Ophuls' song *Murmeln* in the anthology *So Weit Scharfe Zung Reicht,* edited by Klaus Budzinski.

1965 Claude Beylie: *Ophuls,* in *Anthologie du Cinéma,* No. 5 (Paris).

1966 Ophuls retrospective at the Berlin Festival.

Cahiers du Cinéma in English No. 1, published the Ophuls essay entitled *My Experience.* French TV programme on Ophuls in the series *Cinéastes de Notre Temps,* directed by André D. Labarthe.

A Max Ophuls Prize was given by the Nantes Film Society.

1967 *Filmkritik* reprinted a series of articles by Ophuls (in March) and followed this up with a critical essay (in May).

1968 Victor Perkins directed a schools-TV programme (BBC) on *Letter From An Unknown Woman.*

1969 *Lola Montes* script was published in the series *L'Avant Scène du Cinéma,* No. 88.

1970 Howard Koch, scriptwriter for *Letter From An Unknown Woman,* published *Script to Screen with Max Ophuls,* in *Film Comment,* Vol. 6, No. 4. The National Film Theatre in London organised its second Ophuls retrospective.

1971 *Film Comment,* Vol. 7, No. 2: special issue on Ophuls, with contributions by Andrew Sarris, M. Kerbel, G. Carey, William Paul and Foster Hirsch. This magazine continued publishing essays on Ophuls' films, primarily through contributions by Andrew Sarris.

Publication in *Film Comment* (same issue as above) of Brian Henderson's *The Long Take.*

1973 Alan Williams, *The Circles of Desire: Narration and Representation in La Ronde,* in *Film Quarterly,* Vol. 26, No. 1.

1974 *Monogram* published an analysis of Ophuls' style.

Hartmut Bitomsky's analysis of *Lola Montes* in *Filmkritik* No. 210.

1976 Collective text on *The Family in Reckless Moment,* in *Framework* No. 4, stimulated by Robin Wood's lectures at Warwick University.

Robin Wood: *Personal Views* (London) with essays on *Letter From An Unknown Woman* and *Reckless Moment.*

1977 Radio programme on Ophuls in September, directed by Ulrich Lauterbach, for SWF (Germany).

Filmkritik Nos. 251 & 252: special issues on Ophuls, with a bibliography and numerous texts by Ophuls. *Cinématographe* published a special Ophuls issue.

University thesis (Univ. of New York-Buffalo) by Alan Williams, *Max Ophuls and the Cinema of Desire* (unpublished).

1978 Retrospective at the Munich Cinematheque (Stadtmuseum).

Retrospective at the Edinburgh Film Festival and subsequently at the National Film Theatre, London. Special issue on the director by *Movie (in preparation).* Re-release of some Ophuls-films in Great Britain.

Interview with Max Ophuls

Jacques Rivette and François Truffaut

THE BLUE MAN

Max Ophuls: Let me tell you my first memory of the cinema. I was very young; it was at Worms, during a fair, in a tent. On the screen was a fellow sitting at a desk; he had a headache and seemed quite crazy; he was writing something and smoking nervously. He was in a rage—suddenly he picked up an inkwell and drank the ink; he turned completely blue! This film impressed me enormously because, especially to a child, it was quite unrealistic and just like a fairy story. How can you turn completely blue by drinking ink? I must admit that, when I got home, I had a try. I drank some ink; only my tongue went blue . . . nothing else happened. And that's the first thing I remember about the cinema.

Much later, when I was in theatre—I'd wanted to act, but had become a director, by chance and without much success—I used to see silent films from time to time: I particularly liked those of Fritz Lang. I always found myself drawn to films which were absolutely non-naturalistic. But, even though I was an admirer, a 'fan'*, of Murnau because he was doing what I hardly ever dared dream of—I didn't want to be in movies; I didn't think I'd be capable of it, being so much a man of the theatre . . . I'll tell you a story about Murnau. Have you seen *Faust?* Isn't it fantastic? Well, Murnau was doing some screen-tests in Berlin, because he hadn't yet found his Gretchen. A young girl came to double for the actresses—but only for their legs, because hers were very lovely. One day she was doubling, I think, Lil Dagover's legs and she had been given shoes that were too tight. But as she was getting 5 marks for doubling legs (that is 2 more than for ordinary doubling) and she needed the money, she suffered in silence and stoically accepted the fact that her feet were being crushed by these shoes. A man passed by; he came back, looked at that long suffering face. It was Murnau and Camilla Horn. Later she appeared in commercial films, then disappeared. But it's a nice story . . .

Then, I saw the first 'talkie' at Breslau. I think I've already described the scene to you—Hans Albers lighting a cigarette, the sound of him striking the match, the applause of the public. Now I thought that the moment had probably arrived when we would be needed; when those who weren't used to making actors deliver their lines properly, who knew nothing about speech, would be made obsolete by this new development.

Yes, I thought that I had something to contribute, but I still had some doubts. I never thought that this would become my occupation, and I didn't dare to think that I might work in Berlin. It was too big. I'd been there once, as an actor, but I soon left because that huge town frightened me. It was an incredible coincidence that brought me back to Berlin: a theatre troupe who specialised in political plays came to Breslau. They attended rehearsals of a

*In English in the original.

play I was putting on there, and invited me to direct a play at their theatre in Berlin. One of the company was a young actor who played bit parts and I fell in love with her. Quite by chance, while I was trying to find ways to stay near her after the completion of that play, I met a man who said to me: 'I've engaged a young director who speaks appalling German, and I need another young director to take care of the dialogues.' I took up his offer while in between times I was lucky enough to be able to put on three and four other plays in Berlin. And that's how I became asistant director to Anatole Litvak.

This was the period at which the cinema was developing: young people were in demand, they were sought out everywhere and offered exceptional opportunities. After a week or a fortnight, the producers saw the rushes of the film on which I was the assistant. I was summoned to an office: 'Would you like to make films?' I replied that I wasn't sure that I could, because so far I'd only been concerned with the dialogues. 'We think you can.' I was told to go and look in the studio library for a subject that I liked. Rummaging among the books, I found a work by Kästner, a poet I much admire. Beside me, a young man said: 'What a pity that you took that book: it's the one I was going to choose.' That young man, a beginner like me, was Billy Wilder.

COD LIVER OIL

JR/FT: This must have been the period when Wilder was working with Siodmak?

MO: Yes . . . after that even. I remember the man who'd given me the chance to make films telling me: 'We're very lucky: there's a young journalist, Robert Siodmak, who's just finished a film in which we have every confidence: *Menschen am Sonntag (People on Sunday).* Once I'd been taken on, I had to learn the business and to correct my mistaken notions of how films are made. I was taken to a studio: I saw a woman on a staircase, terribly beautiful, far too beautiful, who was saying: 'Good, agreed. Thursday at 9 o'clock, but be on time.' She said this into nothingness and I couldn't understand why she didn't have a partner standing opposite her or at her side. It must have been eleven in the morning, I think. Then I was shown laboratories, montage rooms, the carpentry workshop and so on and so forth. In the evening I returned to the studio and there, still, was that over-beautiful woman, on her staircase, saying: 'Good, agreed. Thursday at 9 o'clock, but be on time!'

JR/FT: What was the subject of the Kästner that you chose?

MO: He wrote a masterpiece of a children's story, *Emil and the Detectives.* The subject I chose was a fairy tale; without really noticing it, I was always drawn to those sorts of subjects. The title could be translated roughly as *I'd rather have Cod liver Oil.* It's about some children who, each evening, swallow their cod liver oil and say their prayers before going to sleep. One evening, when the room is quite dark, the youngest makes a rather daring prayer: he asks why it's always children who must obey their parents; wouldn't it be possible, once a year, to reverse the roles. The prayer goes up to Heaven: God is out, but St Peter is there, just about to fall asleep, and he asks himself why he, too, shouldn't grant a prayer. He goes into a machine-room full of complicated instruments, and exchanges the cards marked 'parental authority' and 'filial obedience'. The child wakes up with a cigar in his mouth and dressed like a man. He gets up as if everything were normal, goes into his parents' room, wakes them up and sends them off to school. The parents have forgotten all they knew, they are incapable of the least effort and too awkward to manage any gymnastics; for their part, the children go to the office, have to cope with the tax collector and a workers' strike with all the attendant problems, and by the evening they are ready to demand that everything be put back as it was. I made a 25 to 30 minute film about this . . . for three months they delayed releasing it because it wasn't really very good.

Next was *Die Verliebte Firma:* it's about a group of movie people who go off to shoot a film on location and the whole thing goes very badly. Everyone in the team falls in love with the young telegraph operator; they think she can replace the star, who is completely lacking in talent. So they take her with them, because they're all in love with her, and it's very amusing because, at the studio, they love her so much that they all became liars because although she may be very beautiful, she has absolutely no talent either. Finally, she doesn't replace the star, she gets married. It was a fairly insignificant subject, but it's the first film where I felt myself carried along from beginning to end, my first attempt at imposing a rhythm on a film.

AND THEN THERE WAS LIEBELEI

And then, *The Bartered Bride.* Do you know *The Bartered Bride?* It's a masterpiece of straightforward naiveté. If Jean Renoir had been a composer, perhaps he would have written *The Bartered Bride.* In this film there was an extraordinary comic [Karl Valentin], who played the part of the circus director. Let me tell you about him rather than about me. He simply could not learn the words of a written text: you had to explain the scene to him, put his wife there to play whatever part was required and let him improvise the situation. The dialogues which he invented are fragments of great literature, they come from the heart, with humour rather like Schweik. He identified terribly with the role; did I tell you that he played the circus director? Well, he would start around 10 o'clock. One morning I arrived about 9 to see if everything was ready. I found him in front of the tent we used as part of the set, in the process of sticking up a notice on which he had written: 'Anyone who damages this tent will be punished!' He lived in the world of the film, in the spirit of an Eulenspiegel, cruel, but not heartless. One day—it was in 1931—I chewed a piece of grass in his presence. He told me: 'It's bad to eat grass because of the germs.' Some years later, in '33 or '34, I received a postcard onto which was stuck a cutting from a Bavarian newspaper: 'Yesterday, a farmer died at the village hosptal. He had to have his tongue cut out because he swallowed grass.' Signed: 'Best wishes, Paul'. Under the Nazis he was imprisoned several times because, as a circus performer, when he left the ring in the evening, he would raise his arm for the Hitler-salute and shout: 'Heil . . . heh . . . heh . . .! scratchig his head as if trying to remember the man's name.
JR/FT: Did you choose to make *Liebelei?*

MO: Well, I got a telephone call from a producer while I was shooting *The Bartered Bride.* I liked the play a lot and, when I reread it, it seemed a little dusty, but I liked it even more. So I went to see the producer who told me that it absolutely must not be a sad film and that he would agree to the project as soon as a 'happy end' could be found. He could well imagine, he said, some of the scenes being set in a palace, and he told me all this because those were the days of the *The Congress Dances**, of the triumph of Viennese operetta. I was still very young and that first interview ended very badly; I still remember the expression of distress on the face of the secretary as she looked at me when I left the office, and I know the traces of that ordeal must have been written all over my face. That afternoon, I received a telephone call from the distributors, who asked me to come and see them; they knew that I hadn't been able to agree with the producer, so they proposed that I should make the film directly with them. It was written very quickly, in three or four weeks . . . It's funny, I'm often asked to make another film as simple, calm, tranquil as that one. I don't believe I could do it any more, but I've never found another theme which had that sense of calmness to it . . . .
JR/FT: Was the French version of *Liebelei* completely different?
MO: No. I arrived in Paris broke, and agreed to make a mixed version since dubbing had not yet been perfected; and this was the version shown in the principal cinemas. We only reshot the close-ups; the rest was the German version dubbed into French. In all, it took twelve days of work.
JR/FT: Why did you find it so difficult, after *Liebelei,* to film subjects that you liked?
MO: Yes, there really was a break after *Liebelei.* It was very difficult to find subjects which were . . . let's say, poetic. I think that I had an opportunity in France, with *Werther,* but I made a mess of it.
JR/FT: We don't know *Werther,* but we have seen *Yoshiwara* . . .
MO: You shouldn't have . . .
JR/FT: And *Sans Lendemain.*
MO: Not bad. I think *La Tendre Ennemie* still holds up.
JR/FT: And your Dutch film, *The Trouble with Money?*
MO: I think that it holds up too. It was quite interesting. A minor bank employee is carrying a portfolio filled with money; he meets an old friend, formerly a tramp, but now a hotel porter. They walk a little way together and, in the evening, the money has disappeared from the portfolio. The porter is suspected, but cannot be convicted, because the money can't be found. There are some people who believe he is the one who has the money and that, therefore, he must be terribly intelligent, because he had succeeded in emerging scottfree from his trial. So they take other monies to him and he becomes very rich. At this point, the money which really had been lost, is found. He is irritated, because he senses that people have lost confidence in him; he speculates rashly and ends in poverty. That's roughly the story.
JR/FT: At this period, you made films in Holland, France and Italy. Did you move from one country to another because you were asked to?

*An immensely successful musical film by Erik Charrell (1931).

MO: I was invited to Italy. The man who asked me to come was a newspaper proprietor who had seen *Liebelei* and wanted to make a film of a novel he was very fond of, and that he had serialised in one of his newspapers. This man was called Rizzoli. It was his first attempt at cinema. I must say that during those years when I was making films in Italy or Holland, I was in no position to choose.

OUT OF WORK IN HOLLYWOOD

JR/FT: You planned to film *L'Ecole des Femmes* with Louis Jouvet?
MO: Yes. I met Jouvet during the 'exodus' in Aix-en-Provence; I was still in the army. He invited me to leave for Geneva with his company and with Bérard, first in order to save me, then to try to film *L'Ecole des Femmes.* After a few days' shooting, because of lack of money and confidence, the producer abandoned us. It was an experiment for me: I had to follow Jouvet and his actors with my camera during a performance, with an audience present and without trying to make a cinematic adaptation of the play. I wanted to show the actor when he leaves the stage and follow him into the wings while the dialogue is still audible. I wanted to profit from the play of light in front of and behind the footlights, but without trying to show the techniques of theatre. I never moved away from the characters, even when they stopped acting, because that didn't mean they had stopped living. I had scarcely filmed anything except the opening shot: a camera traverses the theatre, over the spectators' heads, and Jouvet, seated on this camera-platform, puts on make-up, transforms himself, unnoticed by the public in the auditorium, as the lights gradually dim. And as the camera crosses the curtain, it vanishes, and Arnolphe remains on stage, alone. This first shot was also the last. Three or four days later, I left for America.

I arrived in Hollywood six months after my demobilisation, at the end of 1941. I crossed America by car with my wife and son and absolutely no one there was expecting me.

In New York, we bought a second-hand car with what funds we had left because, for three, the journey was cheaper that way than by train. After two or three days on the great motorways, the countryside seemed monotonous to me. Later, when I remade the journey, I was better able to perceive the way the landscape differed from one region to another: but, at the same time, it all looked the same. So much so that, after two weeks on the road—we travelled very slowly—I asked in a 'steakhouse' where we'd stopped for lunch: 'How many kilometres to Hollywood?' The waiter replied: 'But you're there!'

From 1941 to 1945, I remained unemployed. I didn't get a single film to make. Of course, I kept in touch with European friends who were more or less absorbed in their own work, and I made contact, through agents, with studio doors which opened very, very slowly. The Americans' attitude towards emigrés, however, was very gracious: they found us interesting and rather exotic, and liked to ask us all kinds of questions. Now, it's different: they only need to spend a day in a plane to come and see for themselves.

I must admit that those four years passed as if it were only one, because every three days or so, someone would say to me: 'You're going to start filming.' One day, a producer I'd known in Europe telephoned me. It was Joe Pasternak, who was going to make *Sentimental Journey,* but the director wasn't in agreement, or he was ill, I can't remember. 'Max, this is it! In three days, you'll begin a film with Margaret O'Brien and Johnny Hof . . . something or other. Stay at home; I'll call you in a few hours.' To this day, I'm still waiting.

A very good agent and one of the most important, Orzati, an old Italian attached to MGM, knew me, because some years previously I'd made a film in Germany with his wife, a Dutch actress. He got to work on my behalf a good deal: he wanted to 'place' me, as the saying goes. One day, he called me: 'I've talked about you to Arthur Freed' (who produces musicals: I love the films he's made with Minnelli) 'Louis B. Mayer (the president) wants to see you at nine o'clock tomorrow morning. It's only a courtesy call. Your salary's already fixed: I wouldn't accept less than a particular sum.' (He cited me a fabulous figure; we were living in one room then, and for that sum we could have bought a castle the next day.) 'Yes, it'll be a courtesy call. We've already talked about you a little, he knows who you are. All you have to say is that you're pleased to be working for him.' The next morning, at 8.45, Orzati and I left his office in a huge limousine and arrived at Mayer's office, which was on the second floor, I think. Orzati said: 'There's Louis B. Mayer's secretary. I'll go in and talk to him for five minutes. Wait a moment for me', and in he went. It didn't even take five minutes; he came out again and said that Mr Mayer hadn't got time, that the meeting had been put off till that afternoon, and I'm still waiting.

Those four years passed like that, very quickly, because I never gave up hope. Every day brought its opportunity which evaporated the next, when a new one took its place. My European colleagues, actors and everyone, never ceased to show me great friendship and solidarity. To put it simply, money goes quickly, and you really need it when you disembark like that, after a war. They made sure that I never lacked funds. There was a sort of aid fund and, later, when I'd earned some money, I always gave a percentage to this fund for those who came after me.

After four years of unemployment, I was able to work, thanks to a friendly gesture—a *great* gesture of *friendship*—by Robert Siodmak . . . No, I'm getting confused with the chronology of events. First of all, I collaborated with Preston Sturges on a film adaptation of 'Colomba': *Vendetta.* They didn't like what I was doing, so this collaboration ended after a few days, and I think that, after me, four more directors worked on that film. It was after this incident that Robert Siodmak telephoned me. That happened just as the war was ending and he said to me: 'If you want to go back to Europe and find work, you must have made at least one film in Hollywood, or else no one will have confidence in you.' Siodmak was much listened to at this time, thanks to the enormous success of *The Killers,* and he did what was necessary to give me a chance at Universal.

And that's how, within a week, I was hired to make *The Exile* with Douglas Fairbanks Jr. Douglas produced the film himself, and I shot it with the greatest possible freedom.

JR/FT: It shows.

MO: Really? I had very little faith in that film. Douglas became a great friend, right from the moment we first met. He told me that this would probably not be the kind of film that people expected of him, but that we would enjoy ourselves. In fact, we did have great fun making the film—perhaps a little too much, because frequently I found myself shooting a scene without knowing who was drawing a sword against whom, why they were fighting, why killing . . . In short, I found it hard to follow. I think that shows in the film, but I greatly enjoyed working with Fairbanks, because in the film he played the part of a very relaxed and joyful man, with a very pure and lively imagination.

JR/FT: Moreover, it's the film in which he is most reminiscent of his father.

MO: Is that so? His father was a real cult figure for him. We spent weekends with him watching his father's old movies, and he told all kinds of stories about him. I think it's a pity that tradition of fairy-tale-like adventure films went out with the talkies. There's much more adventure than fairy-tale in that genre of film nowadays.

JR/FT: You also had fun with the sets: the barge in the Dutch countryside, the windmill . . .

MO: Yes. The sets for *The Exile* were made by a man who had never worked in the cinema before—I can't remember his name for the moment—and who had come from the theatre. Experts kept saying to him: 'But sir, your sets are theatrical.' And he replied, timidly—he was small and very pale: 'Well, why not?' Douglas saw things the same way and I think that comes through in the sets.

During the making of this film, I began to like Hollywood. I wasn't prejudiced against Hollywood, but when you're not working, you don't like the town or country you're living in. When you are working and when it's with people you like, you find the town—Rome, Hollywood, Berlin or Paris—magnificent. And while I was still looking at the rushes each evening, people started talking to me about another project for the same studio: it was *Letter from an Unknown Woman.*

LETTER FROM AN UNKNOWN WOMAN

It was largely thanks to a writer, whose name I'm sure you know, Howard Koch, who was a friend of mine, that the doors of the office of Bill Dozier opened for me. He was the husband of Joan Fontaine and vice-president of the studio, and I discussed the project with him. Before the work could really get under way, we had to win the approval of the company president, Bill Goetz. The president, not just the vice-president. Ah! hierarchies . . . I knew how difficult it was to arrange to meet him, and to be able to speak to him in absolute peace and quiet—the telephone always interrupts a conversation. But there was a turkish bath at the studio and I arranged to take a steam bath at the same time as he did. Naked, in the showers, I tackled him about *Letter from an Unknown Woman.* I told him that I was the only director in the world who could make this film and, shaking his head, he replied simply: 'Why not?' And that was that.

JR/FT: Were you given absolute freedom?

MO: Absolutely. There was a script in existence already, but I got permission to rework it completely, together with Howard Koch, to make it the way I saw it. Since the studio chiefs were very apprehensive, they arranged for a preview. Do you know about previews? The spectators fill in cards which can prove decisive for the film's release. The screening was held in Pasadena, a town near Hollywood. We were terribly eager to know the results, so we waited just by the cinema, under the neon sign of a men's outfitters. Finally, we got the first bundle of cards. One of us read aloud. One card: 'Did you like the film? . . . Not at all. Was the story clear? . . . No ?

The head of the studio drew out the cards one by one. At each 'yes' or 'no', he looked at me, pleased or annoyed, approving or very reproachful. These cards were very detailed, as you will see:

'How did you find the film? . . . Terrific.
Was the story clear? . . . Crystal clear.
And the casting? . . . Brilliant.
The music? . . . Beautiful.
What changes in the cast would you suggest? . . . It was perfect.
What do you think of the theme? . . . Marvellous.
Could you identify with the characters? . . . Absolutely.
Will you recommend this film to your friends . . . Certainly.
Sex? . . . Male.
Age? . . . 9 years.'

It was a very happy production: I had further proof of that only recently. A fortnight ago, Bill Dozier, who hadn't been to Europe for ages, came to Paris and telephoned me here. Like all Americans in transit, he was in bed, a victim of the good food and he hadn't set foot outside his hotel. He told me that the film was having a second career on television. On its release in America, its career had been fairly insignificant: I trembled lest the producers—who had become real friends—would never get their money back. But receipts in Europe were very good and now, it's one of the most popular films on American television. It's a very interesting phenomenon: certain rather intimate films fail when shown in the cinema, but do very well on television.

JR/FT: It's exactly the same with some of Jean Renoir's American films: *The Southerner* and *The Diary of a Chambermaid.*

MO: The Diary of a Chambermaid is a very good film. Marvellous.

JR/FT: They're now doing very well on television.

MO: People who go to the cinema are still thinking about the car they've just managed to park after driving around the cinema ten times. Or they leave the office and take their worries with them, and they are still preoccupied with the activity in the streets which carries over into the newsreels preceding the film. So it can happen that they are not sufficiently relaxed to watch a film which demands all a spectator's concentration. While at home, in an armchair, after dinner, with the lights dimmed, you can achieve that kind of concentration and get involved in the film. That should make us view the future of television with great optimism.

JR/FT: Then you left Universal?

MO: Yes. I worked for MGM. I made *Caught,* which I quite like. But I had difficulties with the production over the script, so that the film goes off the rails towards the end. Yes, the ending is really almost impossible, but up until the last ten minutes it's not bad.

Yesterday, I got a letter from James Mason who wrote to tell me that he had seen the film again on TV, and had found the whole thing perfect except for his performance. At the moment, he's producing a film* directed by a great friend of mine, Nick Ray, who was discovered by John Houseman. Mason would like to make a film in France: I've recommended Becker as director. Mason tells me that he'll film in France on condition that his part of the work is done very quickly and that he's paid a great deal. He states precisely: 'By "paid" I mean given money, and not having my salary used to finance the film—if there is still a company in Europe that you haven't ruined and which is rich enough to give me the exorbitant sum I'm demanding.'

JR/FT: With *La Ronde* you returned to one of your favourite authors?

MO: Yes, and there's a nice thing about Schnitzler's life itself. He wrote *La Ronde* at 23 and *Liebelei* at 40, and you'd think it was the other way round. But when you know his work well, you understand. *La Ronde* is opposed to love and its cynicism is not the fruit of lived experience. But at 40 or 45, Schnitzler is nostalgic for purity and that's why—because he's experienced it—the purity in *Liebelei* is genuine. If he'd written *Liebelei* at 23, he would have infused it with far too much romantic melancholy, whereas at 40 he could view his subject from the necessary distance. That's why I find that *La Ronde,* despite the cynicism of a 23 year old, has a splendid purity and freshness, when he wrote that play, he stipulated that it should not be performed. It was meant to be read.

JR/FT: Nevertheless, it has been staged?

MO: Yes, later. It's being performed now in America: thanks to the film there's been a demand for the play. It's made up entirely of a series of scenes: there is no master of ceremonies. That character was my cinematic invention.

LOLA MONTES

JR/FT: When *Lola Montes* was released, everyone was taken by surprise. Were you not surprised by the film, or at least at the fact that everyone was surprised?

MO: Let me tell you exactly! I was surprised to be taken for a revolutionary, or a renovator, because I thought that all I'd done was the most normal thing

*Bigger Than Life (1956).

in the world. I assure you that there isn't a single element of research in *Lola Montes*—I was really involved in the subject, and still am today. I can assure you that when I was watching the rushes and the projection people said to me 'That blue! That red! It's too daring!', I didn't understand. Everything good in *Lola* happened because of my inexperience with colour and cinemascope—when I looked through the camera's viewfinder, it was as if I'd just been born: I did everything just as it presented itself to me. There was one thing I was very afraid of: the dissolve. I'd made a mistake, which I tried to rectify. When you say 'dissolve here', you must know what colours that's going to produce. When you dissolve a blue sky into a yellow table, there's a moment when the colours mix together—you have to take account of that, or you're in for an unpleasant surprise. During the making of the film, I came to understand that; so I would end scenes on a particular colour and start the next on the same colour. But it isn't always easy to do that. The dissolve constitutes an impressionistic moment and, if you understand that, and keep in mind the dissolve as well as the scene itself, you can obtain extraordinary effects. You know, it's the first film to earn me so many letters, especially from young viewers. Anne Vernon pleased me very much by ringing me to say that, at the Circus Festival, she'd been chatting to a top-rank circus rider and a horse-trainer who'd talked to her for a long time about the circus in *Lola.* They said they found it stunning, just like the circus of their childhood dreams. What they didn't say was 'that doesn't exist, you don't do that in the circus'. I was delighted. *Lola Montes* made me want to narrate stories I will have to struggle with in order to master them. Even if I'm wrong, I'm so pleased with the path I'm following that I want to go on, at all costs. But people won't trust me. No one's going to let me make another film like that. Now, I've got to make a very 'safe' film and then another . . . less 'safe'. At this point, also, I'm telling producers: 'I advise you to make my next film, but not the one after that!'

Yesterday, I saw the English version of *Lola,* which they tried to make behind my back while I was on holiday in Germany. The attitude of the director-general of Gamma Films was most suspicious, even then; he kept phoning me to say: 'Have a good rest, please, do take a rest!' I've seen the cuts—it's incredible to think that people who do that not only have no respect for your work, but they can't even read. In the heyday of the theatre in central Europe, if you wanted to be a theatre director, to have the right to engage artists and be in charge of a theatrical enterprise, you had first to be accepted by the writers and actors themselves. They then granted you what was called an 'artistic concession'. That eliminated the theatre director who was no more than a business man. The production company that was responsible for *Lola* didn't want the film, they never understood it.

JR/FT: Hadn't the same thing already happened with *Le Plaisir?*

MO: To a certain extent, but though they had difficulty financing the film, they did a lot for it afterwards. Those who put up the money for *Lola* were never familiar with the film and were surprised by it. It seems to me that, despite such a stormy passage in France, it's going—slowly— to recoup its

money. There have been astonishing results in Germany: it's in its fifth week in Berlin. It could prove a success in England if it doesn't get distributed by one of the small companies, because these small companies make their profits from French soft porn films. In Germany, the film has been granted a special tax-reduction because of its artistic merit.
JR/FT: Was the King of Bavaria's *'ça ne va pas'* ('It doesn't work') on the stage at the theatre the result of a faulty take?
MO: Not exactly. During the first rehearsal, when I told him to cross that bit of the set, he naturally hesitated. I told him he must be getting old, but that we could keep that bit of business in, since it fitted the part of a king.
JR/FT: And wasn't the actor the one who played the painter in *Liebelei?*
MO: Yes. We were young then.... There was trouble with women all the time: to marry or not to marry, to separate or not to separate. During *Liebelei,* he was living with a woman artist who was always making scenes and he told me: 'I'm going through a crisis. I want to live alone, but it's very difficult.' I asked why he didn't leave her and he said: 'One of the reasons is that I don't know who'd bring me my cup of cocoa when I get up in the morning.' Time passes; he marries for the eighth time, but I hear little of him. Emigration comes, France, war, America. During the war, someone from Germany comes to see me and says: 'I'm to give you Bernard's best wishes. He says to tell you that now, there's no cocoa any more.'

I also knew the 'ear doctor'. He's 83 now, and a former juvenile lead in the theatre. As a spectator, I'd greatly admired him and never dreamt that one day I'd work with him. Nowadays, he lives in Munich. He's very fond of wine, so, in order to make him play his scene and move around the set, we hid glasses of wine everywhere. That's why you see him drinking halfway through the scene, where he's talking about Mozart. We placed a glass at each point, so that he'd remember that was where to go. After the shooting, I asked him if the wine was good: 'I couldn't tell you this evening. I've drunk too much.'

THE TERM 'BAROQUE'

JR/FT: When speaking of *Lola Montes,* many people have used the term 'baroque'. Does this astonish you?
MO: For me, the word 'baroque' signifies an architectural period and I find it difficult to say when it begins and when it ends. I remember saying once: 'That's Renaissance', and being told: 'No, it's Empire!' I think the word itself has undergone a transformation when people use it today. I don't know exactly what they're trying to say when they use it. Do they, for example, mean 'voluptuous'? I'm familiar with Austrian churches which I'm told are baroque. That baroque I find charming: it reflects the sun, it is truly musical and gives a certain dignity to the surroundings. But I don't know what is meant exactly when it's used for films. I could understand if it were used to describe certain parts in a film which correspond with what I've just told you. But otherwise . . . I don't know why they use it. Do you?
JR/FT: Perhaps it's being used very loosely to mean that the baroque is a

blend of lightness and gravity, in the sense that one says, for example, that Mozart is a baroque musician.
MO: In that case it's obviously meant as a compliment . . . a compliment that frightens me a little!
JR/FT: Certain critics reproached you for the interior decor of your Norman Church in *Le Plaisir.*
MO: It's most amusing. d'Eaubonne first did a series of sketches – he's a man I adore and admire enormously, in spite of his terrible temper. He brought them to me and I said: 'But look, you've made a mistake; that could be an Austrian church!' He said: 'Except that my church is composed of a church in Spain, near the village of x . . . , close to the French border, and a Norman church.' That dispelled any lingering doubts on my part, because I found these sketches ideal for what was going to take place in the church in *Le Plaisir* – there, you are right, the serious wedded to the light. I accepted them and we filmed it. Then I went to look for locations in Normandy because it was there that I shot the scenes in the countryside. Sometimes I read: 'Why did he shoot this film in the Tyrol? . . .' We found the right place which also had a church. We opened the door and, inside, it was almost exactly like that in the film – naturally, because church architects frequently travelled and borrowed ideas left, right and centre.
JR/FT: Didn't you give d'Eaubonne specific instructions about the style you wanted?
MO: No. I never ask for a realistic or any particular style. I tell him the story and explain the mood of each scene, then d'Eaubonne does the designs as he sees them. I work very, very well with him, because he understands.
JR/FT: Perhaps you already had the idea for the angels before the models were made?
MO: The angels? Ah, yes! . . .
JR/FT: Do you prefer to work in the studio or on location?
MO: I'm not sure. Locations would perhaps be better, if you could manipulate the weather the way that a painter gets the landscape he wants in his picture. If only, when I'm filming, the landscape, weather and the atmospherics would all do me the favour of applying themselves to the story. Since this rarely happens, I don't usually shoot on location. But there is nothing so beautiful as being surprised by nature's kindness. I had an extraordinary piece of luck, for example, in *Le Plaisir* . . . .
JR/FT: With the beach?
MO: Yes. If all locations proved as co-operative, it would be marvellous.
JR/FT: We asked you that question, because some of your films were shot entirely in the studio—*La Ronde,* for example.
MO: Yes, of course. I'd already filmed one shot on location for *La Ronde,* but I cut it. It was in the episode with the poet and the actress. They spend a night in a hotel, and the Master of Ceremonies—who has taken them there in a sledge—waits outside in the snow, while his feet are freezing.

The truth of the matter is that I don't believe in cinematic adaptations which try to break up the action, usually by alternating interiors and exteriors.

Instead of having a character say: 'I'm a little late because the taxi couldn't move', you have to show the motionless taxi. I don't believe in that. I believe in locations only in so far as they cohere with the rest or are used for dramatic shock; they must be treated like a dramatic colour and not used at the whim of realism.
JR/FT: We find this 'location-shock', for example, in the *Maison Tellier* episode of *Le Plaisir.*
MO: Yes, that's right. 'Location-shock' can be extremely interesting.
JR/FT: When you talked about Schnitzler earlier, you insisted on the purity of his work. Very often, this sense of purity is to be found in your films, in *Le Plaisir,* or in *Letter from an Unknown Woman.*
MO: I can't really explain it to you. The theme of purity may not be immediately apparent in a subject, but the story can develop towards that conclusion. A conclusion that has no explanation, that certainly doesn't find its explanation in real life.

I'VE ADMIRED BALZAC FOR YEARS

I rang Louise de Vilmorin to see if she had a subject for me. She sent me a copy—with a beautiful dedication—of her latest novel, *Histoire d'Aimer**. Have you read it?
JR/FT: Yes.
MO: There's another example. Perhaps it's dangerous to want to judge oneself, but I'm sure I'm not a moralist. Maybe I'm always looking for that beautiful purity even without knowing it. It's the most wonderful thing when you find it. And it's there, in this novel.
JR/FT: It appears to be difficult to adapt.
MO: No, no, easy. If I do it, you'll see why. Very easy!
JR/FT: Histoire d'Aimer seems to be Louise de Vilmorin's lightest novel, but in fact it's the most serious.
MO: Exactly. Someone said to me: 'Listen, I can't believe it; this novel is appallingly banal', but it was just the same with *Lola Montes:* depth hiding behind banality. She was incredibly courageous to write this book, because, at first sight all it is is two women talking, with death—so close to love—in the background. The two interrelate, you can't get away from it. One day I may make *Tristan and Isolde* . . . . That young man who lives on a tomb, the about-turn of the ending, everything is extraordinarily forceful. I find it very hard now to decide on a topic, because I know that my answer to certain complaints from the industry must be to make a film cheaply. The subject of *Histoire d'Aimer* could be just right for me.

And I must tell you: I've read *The Lily in the Valley* at last! There's a complexity in the man's emotional life that I like very much. Often, it's quite close to Musset in its melancholy and is different from the Balzac I knew. I love this novel, I can't say why. It's the same with Schnitzler, for example: I *see* each thing, that's all. I see it at once, and not in two different ways: I see how it has to be. And that's a terribly rare sensation when you read a book. You can

*This title can be translated as *A Matter of Loving.*

understand it, you can follow the story, but you don't see it. And in this case, it's as if Balzac was already a film director: he dictates the images with such visual clarity that it's quite astounding, there's no room for discussion. Unfortunately, no one will want to let me make this film now, because it would be too expensive.

JR/FT: You'd make it in the Touraine, on real locations, with only a few characters.

MO: Yes, but which Touraine? You'd have to wait until it was exactly right for the story, wait till the sky was the right colour. And the world in which the story takes place is so luxurious! . . . It can't be done. You couldn't ignore Felix's childhood: it's absolutely crucial. It has to be shown, and the psychoanalysts could always come and learn something there.

I have to admit I read it in German, because in French one or two words might still escape me. Sometimes you come across a difficult word. I read and at the end of the page I think I've understood, but often I risk not sensing the full beauty of a word. Whereas in German, I can be sure that nothing escapes me. So I read that Felix sees castles and towers, and is constantly wondering if she lives in that particular tower. When he discovers her for the first time, I know that it is in very, very long shot, that he discovers her behind a latticework of foliage, wearing a pure white dress.

JR/FT: You already see the framing?

MO: Yes, it's written that way.

JR/FT: What about their meeting?

MO: That shoulder? It's unbelievable! It has an irresistible sensual force.

JR/FT: Yes, but how would you do it so that people don't laugh?

MO: I'll tell you something terrible: if they laugh, it's just too bad! No, perhaps that's wrong: if you don't take it into account, perhaps there's a chance they won't laugh. But if you give it too much consideration, you run a grave risk of making a mistake. Really, I haven't read anything so exciting in years. Any film I make now instead of this one will be inferior, and probably this is one I'll never make. In that novel, there's a dose of realistic detail which is splendid, musical. When Balzac talks about politics, about Napoleon etc . . . realism plays its true role. It upsets and slows down the dramatic flow. You have to concentrate your forces to touch the heart; it's there, between that desire to touch the dramatic nerve-ends and your emotions: and it slows things down. It is its only dramatic function and it's splendid. When you dare to use it like that, you get an unbelievable control. It's like in a symphony, when you separate emotional truth from the truth of life. Such skill is unbelievable . . . so powerful!

I've long been an admirer of Balzac. Before, when I read *La Duchesse de Langeais,* I loved the way he had the people subjected to the pressure of political events: his characters are always splendidly indecisive. When they're flung about from one side to the other like that, they always give us the impression that they're helpless victims. In Balzac, men often put on a poorer show than women in the face of political events. The women still carry conviction probably because they're not so closely linked to politics: they have

the courage to form an opinion. The men are just opportunists.
JR/FT: You mentioned Musset on the subject of *The Lily in the Valley.* You're going to put on some of Musset's comedies in Germany, aren't you?
MO: Yes, I'm starting on that very soon. I have a secret penchant—radio. I love radio plays: everything that can't be done in the theatre or cinema, I'm going to try to do on radio. A couple of years ago, at Baden-Baden, I did a radio programme. I also adapted a work by Goethe called *Novella*—it's wonderful. Now, I'm working on a short novel by one of my favourite authors, Schnitzler again. So far, I haven't been able to find a producer for a film. I thought I might be able to in Germany.

I'm also going to translate several of Musset's plays in German. I've discovered a gap in theatrical cultural exchange. Musset is unknown in Germany and he is never performed. If I can get him accepted into the German theatrical repertoire, even if my work is very modest, I think he will become recognised and be performed very, very often, because Musset is very close to Büchner. I've always said that with *Léonce and Léna* and *Fantasio,* it was as if you heard the bells of an Alsatian church from across the Rhine. There is a distance between the two, but it's minimal.

I also feel that Mozart, for example, is ideal for television. Some of his themes have elements of the unreal in them, as in *The Abduction from the Seraglio* or in *Cosí fan tutte.* It is one of the rare occasions when you gain in artistic effect from the limitations of a small screen. The instrumentation, which is so subtle, is equally suited for television.
JR/FT: For a long time you've had a project to make a film not *of Don Juan* but rather *around Don Juan?*
MO: Yes, I wrote the story: I got as far as doing the script with Peter Ustinov. It wasn't me, but other people, who abandoned it. It was the story of an opera singer who sings *Don Juan* at Saltzburg and who has the same adventures in real life. It was to have been an English production. Since we're on the subject of music, I met someone a week ago and said to him that it would be interesting if Europe could contribute in its way to the musical film, as the American films have done. He wanted to know what with. I said: 'With any Offenbach, that really is the music of my life'. 'But Offenbach isn't French!' this person replied. Isn't that monstrous?

AESTHETIC PATIENCE

I read an article . . . I can't remember where, an article by Hitchcock about the refrigerator-public—a very good piece. It's unbelievable, the public scarcely exists any more. They're a mass of consumers, that's all. The danger is that you see too many films. It's a danger I've avoided because I've found a novel excuse for hardly ever going to the cinema—if the film is by a director I really admire, I can imagine it for myself. When you're familiar with the style of a great director, you can picture the film so clearly that there'd be no point in going to see it. You can also imagine the films of those whose work is awful. But often, people simply see too many films. In America, you start at twelve years old, you watch films then 'till you're twenty and that is how you become a consumer. Consumers watch films the way they stick a cigarette in their mouths: they're no longer aware that they are smoking, they keep it in while they talk.

A few days ago, I saw *Si tous les gars du Monde**: towards the end, the boat on which all the action takes place returns to port. In the harbour, people are waiting, they see the boat, they cheer it, the music swells and the public rises, without waiting for the closing shot. There's the proof that they are consumers.

It doesn't matter which of my colleagues it happens to: it marks the collapse, downfall, death of his craft. Go to a concert: even Mr. Beethoven goes 'pom, pom, pom-pom . . . pom, pom, pom, pom, po-om, po-om . . .' ten times. No one gets up. As for consumers, I mingle with them and listen. Well, I can tell you, one is wasting one's time—they do your job much better and much more quickly. It starts at the first step on the stairs: 'Well, I thought that . . . and the other one . . .' And they begin to take apart what they've seen. They are no longer individuals ready to receive, they're just people who come and consume, and destroy what they have just consumed. How quickly it happens! Between their seats and the exit they've discussed the whole thing. It's quite finished. They never refer to it again. As a result of this continuous mass production of dramas, with people to consume them who see six or eight such works every month, it's impossible to appreciate a really 'dynamic' film. It's like newspapers: they can't publish poems; and people read maybe three or four papers a day . . .

I shall never in my life forget the way that crowd got up: it wasn't because they hadn't been involved in the film—quite the contrary. It's just that aesthetic patience no longer exists.

*Directed by Christian-Jacque, 1955. English title: *Race For Life.*

Reprinted from Cahiers Du Cinema, *No. 72, June 1957. Translated by Jennifer Batchelor.*

The Pleasure of Seeing

THOUGHTS ON THE SUBJECT MATTER OF FILM.

Max Ophuls

Editorial note: *The German title of this short essay is* Die Lust Am Sehen, *which poses a number of problems for the translator. First, 'Lust' means 'desire' but also 'pleasure', as in, 'pleasure principle'. In this translation, 'pleasure' has been used except where the context required the term 'desire'. A second problem is Ophuls' predilection for puns. Throughout the article, Ophuls plays on the polysemic aspects of the German word 'Geschichte', which means both 'history' and 'story' (cf. the French term 'histoire'). Efforts have been made to retain the double meanings, even if this meant putting considerable strain on the English language in the process.*

The story of a film is a riddle. I find it difficult to write about, because if one defines something full of secrets its beauty may be destroyed. Thoughts about this were going through my head this morning while I was shaving, but wishing to resolve the fascinating riddle. A film story only exists for me when I can visualise a succession of images; and this does not happen very often. What prompts me to do so can be almost anything: a novel, perhaps a play, or even a poem. It can start with something that happened to me, or an event that someone recounts to me; it can start as a day-dream, or it can come from a piece of music, or from looking at a picture. The inception of a vision is everywhere and nowhere at all.

Just one thing seems certain to me—that one ought not to be completely certain that one has found the story for a film until one feels that this vision is unalterably fixed in a succession of images or before one feels in one's self the almost physical desire to bring this sequence of images onto the screen. I'm not a writer—much less a poet—but I can well imagine that they are just as perfectionist about a word or a verse or about the way that one scene leads into another, as someone who makes films is about the way his images succeed one another. The masters of our profession, Rene Clair or Jean Renoir, for example, Jacques Becker in his late work, or John Ford in many of his early films, in their best moments of 'in-sight' transcend both dramatic structure and dialogue, and create a new kind of tension which, I believe, has never existed before in any of the other forms of dramatic expression: the tension of pictorial atmosphere and of shifting images. They have the same impetus and produce the same beauty and excitement that can be found in the pure procession of words in the classical theatre, where logic is thrown overboard, over the footlights, so that it is the sound and rhythm of the words alone which inspire and maintain the spectators' belief in the action. Just as in the theatre the lighting, the set, faithfulness to nature and other incidentals must play a subordinate role to the word, so in films the words, the technology and the technique and the logic of the visible must be secondary to the image, subordinate to the vision containing untold wonders within it, which, in the cinema, can be the bearer of artistic truth.

At one time, in Holywood, I was sitting round a table with some very famous film people and Jean Renoir started thinking aloud. That's something he can do, hold forth like an eastern story-teller. His thoughts dart here and there, often without apparent connection, as if someone were to dig a handful of coloured stones out of his pocket and toss them at random on to the table as presents for his friends. I have never been in his company without feeling that he has enriched me. And on this occasion, I remember, Renoir said: 'Very often there is no text in my scripts. Once the actors feel that they have been properly put in the picture and thoroughly understand the situation, I let them say what they want to'. . . . 'poor actors', said someone. But 'rich Renoir', I thought to myself (a bit enviously).

And now I've just cut myself shaving. Perhaps because I got carried away by my insistence on the priority of the image. But where would people like us get to if we couldn't get carried away? If my overstatement of the case has just one result—sparking off the desire to see—then it will not have been in vain. For the pleasure of seeing should be the moving force behind my film story. If this pleasure is pure and strong and inflexible and each time born anew, then it can lead to film (hi)story. The person who can really let this feeling grow within himself is a 'seer' and therefore a film-poet.

There are a lot of others who don't see with the heart and eyes but with the camera lens. They are 'script writers', or at best 'assistants to the action'. They produce our industry's spare parts, but will never invent an engine for it. And then there are the seers who lived before our time, those who, I am convinced, would have written for the cinema if only it had existed at the time. They are difficult to find; their names aren't in the telephone book. But you can find them in books such as the Bible, the Koran or in the Arabian Nights. People such as Maupassant and Stendhal.

So where does one look for a solution? Often, in its many crises, it has looked as if film were dying, as if it were stuck up a blind alley.

But could it give up the ghost before it had really lived? Could it just have been an instrument that no one could play? Will people later look back at it and see an organ with many different pipes and stops except that when air was pumped through it, the sounds coming out were seldom music? Could it be that there will never be a (hi)story of film because there were never enough film stories?

Just recently, and this was by no means the first time this has happened to me, I outlined to someone a story that I could clearly see before me and which is close to my heart. Three days ago the idea was passed on to the producers with the request that if they liked it, they should phone me. So far no one has rung.

Perhaps it would have been better if I hadn't shaved today.

(1954)

Reprinted with permission from the Deutsche Zeitung/Christ und Welt, *Vol. 9 No. 47.*

THOUGHTS ON FILM

An Improvisation by Max Ophuls

Cast: Max Ophuls, Marianne Kehlau, Friedrich Schönfelder, Announcer . . . Other Voice . . . Director . . . Tram Conductor . . . Ticket Inspector . . . Man . . . Woman's Voice . . .

Music: Dance—*fades out—mixes into applause*

Voice of Announcer over applause

Announcer: Tonight *Hessischer Rundfunk* is broadcasting an experiment, a paraphrase as we are calling it, of a lecture. We don't know whether the title makes any sense, or even if the entire programme does. It came about like this—a lecture was recently given in Frankfurt by Max Ophuls, the film director. He . . .
Ophuls (interrupting): I didn't give it to talk about myself. It was more because . . .
Announcer: All right, all right . . . Please don't interrupt. We haven't even started yet.
Ophuls: That's just why, if it's all the same to you. I wanted to state before we began that any other director besides me could have given that lecture, and that it wasn't I that was speaking, or is speaking. It was my profession. I dislike personal . . .
Announcer: All right, all right. And so we've used this lecture to put together a radio play of thoughts, passing thoughts, mental reservations, digressions, interludes, opinions and counter-opinions in untrammelled disorder, simultaneously and one after the other. It began in front of the auditorium of the Frankfurt Society for Trade, Industry and Science. The lecture was called, at least this is what it said on the tickets, *THOUGHTS ON FILM.* We had our recording equipment in the hall, a very pre-war, pre-World War hall, a very cultured hall . . .

Bring up applause. Brief applause in the auditorium

Ophuls: Ladies and Gentlemen!
It's not going to be as easy as I thought, I can see.
Schönfelder: Of course it's not that easy. He's got stage-fright, which any director would have in his place, standing so close in front of an audience. Normally directors think of audiences as something anonymous in darkened halls, and now there's one sitting right in front of his nose.
Ophuls: One day I got a letter. Our request is whether you would speak on a similar subject to the one which recently in a newspaper . . . I had written some article or other in a newspaper, to our members.

But after I had agreed I got stage-fright, and happened to read a book by Hermann Hesse, called *Der Kurgast.* And in this book he wrote how one day he had set off on a lecture tour . . . It hadn't bothered him. He'd agreed to do it all over the place. It was in Southern Germany, twenty or thirty years ago, I think. Because after he'd agreed, he'd thought he could always send a telegramme at the last minute, calling it off. And that helped me slowly to approach this lecture, and you and this city.

Schönfelder: Ah, it looks as if it's going better. He's getting over his stage-fright.

Ophuls: Because giving lectures, believe me . . . That's to say, I'm a beginnner at it. I've given perhaps three or four lectures in all in my life—giving lectures isn't an easy thing to do. A gentleman from Frankfurt has said a thing or two about it, and I don't think we should overlook what he says, because I think we listen too little to what he says anyway.

I always listen to him with music—with Haydn's music. Yes, they go well together. And as if it were spoken by a woman, that's how beautiful it seems to me.

I've written down, and am now going to read out to you, what he wrote about lectures. Perhaps giving lectures undermines all that you stand for. But anyway, I've written it down, and I'll read it out. This is what he writes:

Bring in Haydn music
and quotation from Goethe in the new version
spoken by Marianne Kehlau
The first lines of the quotation spoken by Ophuls up to:
. . . to give a lecture.
Then mix in Kehlau's voice which speaks to end of quotation
Quotation behind the music

Why should it be that we, however earnestly urged, are so reluctant to decide to give a lecture on a subject about which we are well informed.

We have carefully considered it, we have assembled all our material and have put it in order as well as we could. We have withdrawn from all possible distractions and when we pick up our pen we put off starting it. It could be because man is not a teaching being, but a being of life, action, decision.

Music fades out

Ophuls: The gentleman who wrote that was called Wolfgang von Goethe. In my nervousness I then tried to find out about you. I wanted to know whom I should be talking to. They told me it would be gentlemen by and large, sometimes ladies were allowed, but by and large it would be gentlemen who had had a hard day's work, most of them didn't come, and those that came were normally so tired that they certainly didn't want to listen to a lecture. I don't want to give one. You don't want to listen to one. I think this is a good time for us all to be allowed to leave.

But I think it's probably a good basis for nibbling away at some thoughts, touching on some, perhaps simply following a few trains of thought, informally if possible. After that—I've just noticed that the lecture hasn't begun yet, after that we exchanged letters about the title, and I'm about to commit a second indiscretion. I'm going to read out to you the letter that I received. It says: When we met in Frankfurt, you kindly allowed us to suggest a subject for your lecture, if one were to occur to us. Here, then, is our suggestion: *The Creation of Film as a Task and a Duty.*

On a tape in the background is heard, perhaps with an echo and like a record repeating itself, spoken by different voices, the words:
. . . as a task and a duty . . .
as an acoustic background to the next three sentences

That was to much for me. I didn't accept this title, because from my earliest youth I had found tasks unpleasant at school. And I refused to do them because they represented a duty.
Mix in
Schönfelder: As he is saying that, his thoughts wander, and a French *bon mot* comes into his head.
Kehlau: A descant on duty.
Ophuls: The Englishman does his duty, the German searches for a duty to do, and the Frenchman does anything but his duty.
Schönfelder: He remembers it, but of course he doesn't say it.
Ophuls: And I always ran for safety to my imagination. It went something like this:

In the third form, at school in Saarbrücken, we had to write a geography essay about the course of the Rhine. And I described the adventures of a drop of rain, which fell into the Rhine at Schaffhausen and then flowed along with it. And as it passed towns I didn't know too much about it felt tired, fell asleep, and let itself be carried on by the water. When we got our essays back, the teacher, the senior master, his name was Dr Lippert, had written at the bottom of mine: This essay does not appear to be worthy of a German third-former.

Running for safety to imagination, was, of course, even then I assume, a little pointer to my profession. But the most interesting pointer, and the pointer to the subject I want to speak about tonight, also comes from my memories of my youth, and, oddly enough, from my memories of Frankfurt-am-Main. I had a grandfather who lived here, and I came to stay with him in my early childhood. It was a matter of pride to him–as to all grandfathers—that his little grandson had learned to read before he had to—something which I can't understand at all. If I were a grandfather, I shouldn't be like that. Because I think we learn how to read quite early enough. At all events at five years old I could read a bit, and we went in tram number 1 or 2 or 3, I think perhaps 4, past the Opera House. My grandfather had a season ticket for the opera. He was a shopkeeper with a shop at Zeil. As we rode past I read out the words—which I read again this evening as I came here in my car—the words on the inscription: Dem Wahren, Schönen, Guten (To truth, beauty, goodness). That evening, over dessert, my grandfather said: Now you just tell us, Max, what you saw today; what you read out; what was it you read out? Because my grandfather was a tradesman, a tradesman who always had been a tradesman, and since I had been brought up to be the same, even at five years' old, I said: I read out *"Den schönen, guten Waren"* (To beautiful, good goods).

This curious mistake actually symbolises my profession. It symbolises film, at least film as it is today. It is the task of people with positions of power in the profession, such as directors like myself and the profession's industrial managers to bring these two attitudes together, to make them merge without the one destroying the other.

Film must be a struggle between the *schönen guten Waren* and the *Wahren-Schönen-Guten.*

If this combination is successful it produces something which, in my opinion, justifies its own existence. If it is unsuccessful and there is a bias towards either of these two attitudes, the situation becomes very dangerous. I shall now review in passing the problems which these two attitudes produce. I'd like us to go past them quickly, so that the tram that runs alongside the Opera House can push on to its destination, and I'd like you to board it with me. Would you care to?

Tram bell

Announcer: Hold tight! Any more fares please?
Another voice: It's an odd lecture, too discursive for me, eccentric . . . too much imagination . . .
Woman's voice: But just as interesting as a proper one, don't you think?
Tram conductor: All aboard.
Ophuls: And now we can touch, in passing, on questions about this industry or this art or this industrial art or this artistic industry without them holding us up. Like everyone who reaches a certain age and who loves his profession, I too have had the idea of one day writing a book.

A book about my profession. It's not that the book should set out to show that I know better than the people who will read it. It's more that it might help me to get some things clear which one has been trying to get clear all one's life if one practises a profession.

I've made some notes for this possible book. And I'll simply read a few of these notes out to you. And perhaps the notes will introduce us to some problems. I find that the most interesting aspect of these problems is not their solutions but—and these are perhaps the only interesting aspects of them—their insoluble elements, their oddities. And I'll read you out a few of these oddities from these cards I have here.
Schönfelder: The director lays his cards on the table.
New voice: Genuine cards?
Another voice: Fake cards?
Yet another voice: They can't all be trumps!

Ophuls: Discovering talent. A mystery as far as I'm concerned. Because it's full of contradictions. Does the unacknowledged genius exist? That is a note to which I don't know whether in our profession there is an answer. Is a career an accident, is it fate, can it be put down to personal energy? I know, for example, that a year or two ago I was driving back into Paris one morning after working on a film.

Bring in: Bells of the Sacre Coeur. Any bells.

We had been filming all night, and in the car with me was a young actress who had had perhaps a total of ten lines, and we drove round the Place de la Concorde, and the sun rose. It was in that kind of light that turned the yellow and grey stones pink and which made it very pleasant to think and chat.

Bring in: Girl's voice in French, so that what Ophuls is saying sounds like a translation. The French voice continues speaking below Ophuls.

tu sais, cette nuit, je me suis décidée . . . si dans un an, ça ne marche pas . . . eh bien, moi, je fais un coup de tête, je te dis, Max . . .

And the girl said to me: Well, I've decided tonight that if I'm not a recognised actress in a year, I'll commit suicide.

I met her again a year later. She was married to an American hotelier. That's the secret of vocation; and the hotelier was beginning to take an interest in financing films. That seems to me to be an even greater secret. This secret of vocation has of course also something to do with us, with us film directors. People demand that we should be discoverers. And to be a discoverer you need something—the profession has a name for it—it's called flair. So we've got good noses, we can smell it out.

Bring in tram sounds

Conductor: Next stop! Do you want to be in the movies?
Golden Bridge . . . Success Street . . . Do you want to be in the movies? *He rings his bell.*
A lot of voices: Oh, yes please . . . yes, please . . . oh, yes please.
Conductor: Don't push.
Announcer: Next problem. Do you want to be in the movies?
Ophuls: Round about 1932 in Berlin, when Berlin was the cosmopolitan theatre and film city which we're still trying to find today—at that time I had a great patroness. She was an actress called Rosa Valetti, to whom I owe a great deal. She had a literary cabaret that came on at night after the theatres had come out. You could hear Spoliansky's music or Holländer's there.

Bring in music on two grand pianos

I got a telephone call one night, and Valetti said to me: 'You're always on the lookout for young people, new faces. I've got someone. You've got to come, you've got to find the time. It doesn't last more than half an hour, so don't be lazy. Come along, come along one night at one o'clock. It's a woman, a little girl. She's not so little, she's good-looking, in fact she's very good-looking. She's singing the third cobbler's boy, it's nothing much. But those few words—well, you'll be able to tell right away, the way she sings them. I've got a feeling she's a great actress'.

And so I went and rang up Rosa Valetti next morning and told her: I listened to her. I don't understand. All right, it didn't last long, but if it lasted longer I'd have felt I'd wasted an evening. The woman who played the cobbler's boy was Marlene Dietrich. That's our flair.

Bring in song by Marlene Dietrich
Only the tune, not the voice

But if we say there really is something as insoluble as vocation, then that leads us to another interesting insoluble problem.
Schönfelder: He lays a second card on the table. He's playing his cards face up.
Ophuls: In a profession such as film is it intuition that is the motor, the thing that takes it forward, or is it the academic element? This is a problem common to all expressive professions that has not yet found an answer. The most interesting and most insoluble part of it for me is contained in an anecdote from the life of Isadora Duncan—Isadora Duncan, who is credited with bringing new life to the dance, with leading it away from classical ballet towards a liberation of the body.

I've discovered that my education is erratic. I only educate myself when I have to make a new film, and have to become involved in the problems which the film poses. I then go into them and find out a great many details. And at one time I was supposed to make a film about Isadora Duncan, and so I worked it out from letters and documents.

Bring in Ballet music A Midsummer Night's Dream

Isadora Duncan was a nice little ballet dancer who helped her mother to make ends meet, and who arrived in Chicago to appear in *A Midsummer Night's Dream.* She was in a Greek toga, came in too late in the second act, couldn't do her shoes up and threw the shoes aside—it would have taken her too long to tie them up. Out she came without her shoes on, in her bare feet, and danced to the music. The theatre rose to its feet and clapped. Probably one of the greatest moments of liberation and spontaneity, intuition and originality. Later Isadora Duncan set up schools in which people could learn how to dance in the original way in which she danced.
Ophuls or announcer: repeating And therefore originality turned into theory.
Ophuls: For me that is one of the problems to which I have no answer at all.

Bring in tram bell

Conductor: Insoluble stop. We're carrying on. No one leave the tram.
Announcer: A new card please.
Ophuls: Without any connection between the notes I've brought along with me, this one says, and it has nothing to do with it, *Cinemascope.* I've written about it and would like to expand on it if it weren't that I'd become too broad.
Announcer (curtly): A rather tatty card.
Ophuls: Another card. Censorship. A favourite topic at film congresses. With free travel, free expenses and free cigars, it's nice to talk about intellectual freedom. I am one of those, and am therefore not often taken very seriously by my colleagues because of it, who believes in censorship. But in an unusual form of censorship. Not in political censorship, but in a censorship against banality, which inevitably leads to the brutalisation of taste. I see the censor's office being staffed only by artists. Entry is forbidden to any and every state authority. I think that for me to argue my view of this kind of censorship comes under the heading of insoluble problems.

Bring in Announcer's text(?)

Ophuls: Criticism is really a secret card. Is criticism necessary? What's a director's attitude to criticism? I believe that if I speak at all on my own behalf I ought to apologise. I feel I am speaking for other directors, not for myself. I should think that if they answered the question truthfully their attitude to criticism would be more or less as follows: A bad review, from which you can learn nothing, you throw away. A good review, from which you can learn nothing, you don't throw away. A bad review, from which you can learn something, you have to keep. And a good review, from which you can learn something, you really do keep.

Bring in

Kehlau: Gunter Groll, writing about the role of film criticism: Criticism should open up new paths. Criticism should clarify. Whatever else it does, whether it praises or tears apart, questions or supports, rages or smiles, the only genuine criticism is the criticism which clarifies. There are three characteristics for good criticism—the ability to clarify , distance from its object, and love of its subject.
Ophuls: And I've underlined that in red and kept it in my library.
Kehlau: Thank you. *Bring in at:* A problem *en passant.*
Tram Conductor—Announcer(?)
Ophuls: A problem *en passant.* Should film have a philosophical or political attitude? My answer—a very personal one—is: should an idividual have one?
A problem. Is film necessary at all? My own answer—Yes!
And here I've got—I can't take it out of my scrapbook—something that I wrote on a ticket for a concert, because it seemed a subject that ought one day

to go into the book. I watched the orchestra while it was playing, which you really ought not to do . . .

Bring in: Brückner, Symphony VII, *middle movement.*

But of course film directors, deformed by their profession, see a great deal. And while the orchestra was playing I though of a title which a great journalist, Alfred Polgar, had once given to a collection of essays. The title was *The Blessing of the Ordinary Man.* I could see the humility and devotion with which the man on the tympany was awaiting his turn to play. And I saw the flautists, and they reminded me in the middle of a Brückner symphony of a strand in my profession, of the ordinary people, the roofers who build our houses in films, the gardeners who plant our flowers, the electricians up in their boxes at 40° Centigrade or some such remarkable temperature—I'm not very good at these things. They are people to whom we owe an enormous amount, and they are unusual people. Because someone who makes a table, or a wall or a door, and knows it's to be pulled down again tomorrow, to be broken up, to be as if it had never existed—such a person is someone who interests us film directors enormously, because he possesses something similar to us that unites him with us. He is attracted by something illogical, by the element of play, by the miracle of imagination which is intangible, which comes and then vanishes.

If he didn't have that, he'd be a proper bricklayer, a proper electrician, a proper painter.

It goes a long way, and this is the interesting problem which exists between the *schönen guten Waren* and the *Wahren-Schönen-Guten.* People who only want beautiful goods from film have to be careful that through industrialisation, through time and motion, through the race for planning they do not suffocate the spiritual element that believes in the miracle that exists inside the industry. Otherwise it runs the risk of becoming lifeless.

In a couturier's which makes its own creations, Kerenska—another White Russian—there was a fur coat. They showed me the coat, and I'd hardly ever seen anthing like it before. It was so . . . it stood there, they couldn't make it lie down, it stood firm. It was so luxurious—its material so simple, that it made your heart skip a beat to look at it. I said: Are you selling it? How much are you selling it for? A little salesgirl, another White Russian, said Yes, it's bound to cost a lot. And she told me the price, probably in marks, let's say 50,000DM. Too expensive, we can't afford that.

Bring in

Woman's voice: (in spite of the fact that I've already spoken her part) (?)
Yes, the coat belongs to an old White Russian lady and . . .
she hesitates
Ophuls: Yes?
Woman's voice: . . . and was worn by her lover you see? When she was still a

young woman he crossed the frozen Volga in it to her, four times, Monsieur . . . and frozen. Well, if the lady were to sell this coat . . . It takes a very great deal of money for a person to let herself be separated from such a great experience.
Ophuls: And I asked whether she thought it could be hired out.

No, she thought, not. She wouldn't dare even to suggest it to the Countess. Hiring it out was an unworthy suggestion. (Then she said: What do you need the coat for? And then I told her it was for this or that film, and told her about the film. Then she said: I'll tell this story to the old lady. And she came back three days later and said: You can have the coat. It doesn't cost anything.) (?)
Woman voice: Yes, that's right. That's what I said.
Ophuls: This miracle of believing in the dreams in our films, in the stories—this is a miracle which ought to be maintained, has to maintained in the face of industrialisation. And the reason why it is so difficult to keep it alive is the current configuration of the industry, which is afraid of the miracle because it's afraid of losing money. If the industry, according to my interpretation, relinquishes this miracle through fear, then one day, before it realises, it will have died.

It is the film directors above all who have to remain loyal to the miracle, humbly loyal to it, and even in our own work we have to respect it. Consequently the problem of film directing is really very simple.

Bring in

Voice: Have you always been loyal to it?
Schönfelder: Who's speaking now? Whose voice is that?
Director: That's the film.
Voice: I, the film, am asking the director whether he has been as loyal to my miracle—as he so grandiosely expresses it—as he demands that other people should be. Honestly? Have you always worked in the light of this idealism? Always?
Director: Not always, but certainly sometimes. I've . . .
Schönfelder: He's . . . made good films and some bad ones. Naturally it goes up and down and down and up . . . like, for example, in a *dance* . . . . . .

Fade out

Voice of Kehlau possibly to dance music:

And at this point an example should occur to him which he's already quoted before in a monograph on film directing. *Pause.* Is he going to quote it?
Ophuls: We have to make the people that we have dealings with believe . . .
Voice of Kehlau: No, it's not occurred to him. In that case we'll have to remind him of it.

Music becomes a violin
(Please select a simple violin passage, no virtuosity.)

Voice of Kehlau after a few bars

Fritz Kreisler, the violinist, was once asked if he could explain the difference between a great virtuoso and a great artist, and he said, the artist loves it a little more.

Ophuls: . . . believe in the same beauty, in the same delight that we ourselves feel when we're putting a film together. To do that we need to let them have their freedom. I myself learnt to respect this freedom from a musician. Musicians in particular have and do impress me a great deal.

(Possible Kreisler-quotation)

Ophuls: There was a rehearsal in Paris. I was still very young at the time, and still believed that I was in a profession that had to ensure that authority was upheld. And so at that time I was an authoritarian director. Then Toscanini took me with him to a rehearsal in the opera in Paris. He had not been there for very many years and on the programme was the Egmont Overture.

Bring up Egmont Overture

This gentleman, already old and somewhat hesitant, entered the great building. The orchestra was all assembled and he said to them:

'You will have played the Egmont Overture very, very often. Would you like to just play it to me as you usually play it? And I'll simply listen.'

They began playing. He changed his position a couple of times, motioned them to stop, and said:

'Perhaps it's a little too weak. I'll just go up to the back row and listen from there.' Then he went and listened from there. 'I think I'd like to go over such and such a bar on page such and such myself. And, totally confident in them, he left the rest until the performance. Of course what he said will have been very important and unique. But what was unique for me was to see an orchestra that evening admiring, respecting and loving this man because of the freedom he allowed them. To approach my profession in that way would produce an insoluble problem because of its conflicts with the necessities in putting a film together, in carrying out the job. A film must be financially accountable, in consequence of which the film industry has produced a great many people concerned with the planned and accounted production of film, who have become experts at it and are called production managers.

(Bring in: possibly tram)
(Ophuls agrees)

Conductor: Inspection please.

Announcer: (against tram noise): The inspector has jumped aboard.

Inspector: No travelling without inspection. Inspection . . . Tickets please . . .

Ophuls: There are plans hanging in our offices which are worked out to the minute—when this, that or the other has to be shot, when this or that actor has first to open his mouth and at what time he closes it. The whole thing is a machine which gets in the way of artistic freedom and intuition. How can we come to terms with it? Someone has written on this subject and I'll read him out to you again, but really it ought not to be me that reads it out. A woman ought to read it out to you, because it's so beautifully written and with such tenderness.

Bring in Marianne Kehlau with Haydn music. Please try to come in on the first words in Ophuls' voice and go out on his last words

Kehlau: The artist rests upon his subject. He unites with it in love. He shares the best of his spirit and his heart with it. He gives it a rebirth. In giving it birth time is of no consequence, because it is a labour of love. What lover can tell how time goes by when he is close to the one he loves? What true artist, then, is aware of time when he is working?
Ophuls: That was written by your fellow citizen, Wolfgang von Goethe.

Technology has reached a stage in our profession where it is a threat to our heart. You can tell that when you ask anything of our technicians nowadays that has not yet been discovered, and which arises from your urge to express yourself. If I am standing in a studio and ask, let's say, for the camera to suddenly start swinging up or to start dancing, I find that the first reaction is a bunch of worried technical faces, which I have to take time to transform into comradely ones. And that has to succeed, and it does succeed for my colleagues who produce great achievements. They have felt that the lens which you screw into a camera is really a substitute for the human eye. What does a human eye do? When is it at its most beautiful? Not when it's inquisitive, not when it's closely examining what it's looking at, when it's got an expression of reality about it.

Bring in.

Announcer (Schönfelder): The director is reluctant to be a naturalist.
Ophuls: I think it's at its most beautiful when it's radiant. Therefore it is the film director's job, a job forever impossible and forever being started anew, to talk to the lens as if it were a human eye. The man who represents the lens in the studio is the camerman. You've got to take him by the arm. You've got to take him for a stroll.

Bring in.

Ophuls: You've got to talk to him. You've got to explain it to him so that he can understand or preferably feel what it's all about. Baudelaire knew all about it long before there were films. He sketched it out in a few moving sentences:

Bring in music by Debussy

Man's voice *deep rough, having had a lot to drink.*

THE WINDOW by Baudelaire.

If you look in through an open window from outside, you don't see as much as someone who is looking in through a closed window. There is no deeper, more mysterious, more fertile, more opaque or more shining object than a window lit by candlelight. Nothing that you can see in the light of day can ever be more interesting than things that happen behind a pane of glass. Within this hole, dark or light, life is lived, life dreams, life suffers.

Across the sea of roofs I can see a mature woman, wrinkled, poor, always a little bent, who never leaves the house. From her face, her clothes, her gestures, from almost nothing I have recreated her story, or rather her legend.

Had it been a poor, old man, I could just as easily have created his.

And I lie down to sleep, proud to have lived and suffered in someone other than myself.

Perhaps you'll ask me: 'Are you sure that your legend is accurate?'

What do I care about real reality when my imaginary one helps me to live and to feel that I exist and how I exist?

Ophuls: You have to treat him like an actor who's about to play a scene. Then he'll listen gratefully and then the lens will begin to be radiant. Just when that is happening, and just when you're walking up and down with him most intensively, someone will turn up from production and say: 'What's gone wrong? Why isn't anything happening?' This industrialisation—which I have to keep reminding myself in my profession is the guarantee, the material side of its existence—it does leave so much out of account. There's a great miracle. The miracle of laziness. There's no room for it any more, and it's such a beautiful miracle.

Bring in (as on page 36) a record

Man's voice: Time is money, time is money, time is money.

The record fades in and out as on page 36 and, properly used, produces curious effects.

Ophuls: They all looked the same. . .
Voice: Time is money, time is money. . .
Ophuls: . . . And why do they all look the same? . . .
Voice: time is money, time is money.
Ophuls: And so we run the risk of getting further and further away from the secret which is FILM. At the current film festival at Cannes one of my colleagues, whom I very much respect—he was a member of the jury—said the following about film:

For the first time I have realised what torture it must be to be a film critic. I had to watch ten films in fourteen days. They all looked the same, the only excitment that I felt was about the presentation. Would the film be in black and white, would it be in colour, cinemascope or vistavision?

And why do they all look alike? Because drama cannot be mass-produced. I did a sum about it a long time ago. If a nation can produce three or four dramatists in a generation it's won the jackpot. If we look back through German history, for example, we can find few such times, and the German nation has produced great dramatists. How can it be possible to produce 150 in one year? We're therefore at best compelled to turn to plagiarism as long as we take full responsibility for it, as long as we copy things that are good and beautiful in our eyes. I shall therefore quickly write my plagiarist's thank-you letters. They are addressed—as telegrams, I can't write them all out, there are so many—to René Clair, to Fritz Lang, to Jacques Becker, William Wyler, Carol Reed, Otto Preminger, David Lean, Clouzot, Billy Wilder, Helmut Käutner.

Bring in: Voice of secretary.
Typewriter fading into morse.

Three extra telegrams to Sir Laurence Olivier. Thank-you letters are also addressed to the past, and so they'll probably have to be night letters and are to go to Murnau, Alexander Korda, Jacques Feyder, Stiller and a man whose spirit, even these days without us being aware of it, streams out of his theatres into every studio in the world—Max Reinhardt. And like all my colleagues I have letters of thanks to write to the nameless people who man the bridge with us and who are our assistants or our script girls or the secretary who, just at the moment when you've done something wrong, suddenly shakes her head.

Bring in Mozart music

Or the people who—much too shyly—come to you in the evening and say Might you try to do it in such and such a way tomorrow?

These people, their contributions, their ideas, never named, never on the posters, are part of the miracle of film. And now I'm coming to the greatest miracle . . .

Schönfelder: He's playing his last card: Hearts.

Ophuls: . . . that I specially planned to deal with tonight, because it said on the letterhead—*Society For Industry*. That is the miracle of money. How does money get into the film industry? It seems to me the greatest miracle of all. It think it is because the money that is invested in the film industry believes in miracles. Because it believes it can double or triple itself, and because it believes in quick miracles. And that is why I think that the miracle money in our industry is a long way short of being good money. Because the money that is put into our industry ought to be patient money, so that we are freed from chasing after the day-to-day money, which comes running behind a public that we're only able to entice into our cinemas on a day-to-day basis. I believe that this public, numerous though it is in the dreams of the quick-return financiers, is a dangerous public. The public we need is the public the theatre has discovered, a public that will stay with us on more than a day-to-day basis, and whose enjoyment doesn't dissipate in twenty-four hours. the overnight success which, up until now, exceptions excepted, the film industry has striven for, has run after, is also a chimera, because, contrary to the industry's frequently held belief, it cannot be counted on. In Hollywood I had the experience at the end of a production (I won't tell you which film, it wasn't particularly good), of seeing the Gallup Poll organisation descending on the studio. At that time Gallup had sold a machine to the studio that I worked for, and the machine operated as follows:

Bring in film sounds
Each time people are mentioned—i.e. four women, a priest, etc, the relevant voices reply . . . yes, sir . . . yes, sir . . . with pleasure, sir . . . here . . . yes, sir . . . *(women, priest, soldiers etc).*

They brought people in in the afternoon. They brought in four women over 50, half a priest, two demobilised soldiers, one airman, a nine-year-old boy, a gentleman of 78, a businessman, a scientist etc.—synthetic America.There were 120 people in all. They were made to sit in a little room, like you are sitting here, and the film was introduced to them. Then a man came in and explained to them what they were to do. He said:

We need your asistance. Your judgement will decide for us whether the film is good, whether we'll release it, let it loose on mankind as it stands, or whether we'll improve it or cut it as you decide. You'll find a knob to the right of your seats. On this knob it says very good—good—boring—very bad. While you are watching the film will you please keep turning this knob.

The knobs were connected to electric wires which were synchronised with the film and recorded the audience's reactions. I stood in a corner at the back and all I could hear was sssssssss . . . Dreadful! When the film had ended, there they had a tape.

Fade out film sounds.

Ophuls: This tape was run alongside the film and I saw people who I normally only saw at a distance behind desks (I always had to sit in front of their desks), very respectable, elegant people suddenly crawling about on all fours, peering at the floor. 122. This says bad. What is it? *I love you.* It's no good. This says good. Come on, laugh. What is it? It's 210. Yes, yes, 210. We'll keep it.

Bring in Announcer.

Schönfelder: As he's telling this story it's possible that behind all the words he's remembering his diary. I once saw a copy of his diary . . . somewhere . . .
Ophuls: Worrying about success, overnight success, had brought the industry

to this pass. Thank God that machine doesn't exist any more. All the same, the desire to be able to predict this desire is a heresy and a violation of the secret element in our profession.

(Conversation between the gentleman (financier) and the director).
Music with echo

Ophuls: From my diary (1st April, 1956).
Met a financier today. A fairly new and fresh one. I hadn't called him—he called me. It's better that way in my experience.

Gentlemen: So, you make films for your enjoyment.
Director (me): Not exactly. It's more that I enjoy making them.
Gentleman: You mean you're in a permanent state of enjoyment?
Director: No. But the pain it causes you makes you happy.
Gentleman: And who—forgive me for being blunt—who will guarantee me that the audience is going to enjoy what you enjoy?
Director (evasively): It's just that you believe you've a heart which can feel for them, insights which you can see for them. In short, talent.
Gentleman: Is there no other guarantee?
Director: None.
Gentleman: None?
Director: None. *Pause.*
Gentleman: And what about your experience?
Director: It's virtually nil in this respect. Success can't be calculated in advance. Yesterday I was going down the Champs Elysées with Henri Jeanson. It's easy to chat on the Champs Elysées. Perhaps that's how it got it's name. And this is what he said to me: 'When Julien Duvivier and I had finished our film *Pepe Le Moco* (and *Pepe,* as you know sir, is one of the most successful films that has ever been made in France), when we saw the first print we were convinced it was a catastrophe. In London we even left the première to avoid being at a disaster.' There you are—your guarantee.
Gentleman: I like you. You're straight. We'll give you all the money you need for your films.
Director: . . .
Gentleman: That's to say, if it's not too much. We assume in advance that as well as your talent you'll also be using your experience. We not only want a good film, we want value for money too.
(He looks in his briefcase, in which he's got a list of things I've done).
Gentleman: You do have experience, don't you?
Director: Yes, a little.
Gentleman: A lot, surely?
Director: A lot of a little. It doesn't amount to anything very much.
Gentleman (suddenly): Colour, for example. What do you think about colour?
Director: If you want it in black and white, the less the better.

Gentleman: And you know all about cameras, sound, editing, design, costumes, script . . . . don't you?
Director (loftily): Like a doctor knows his operating instruments, like a pilot knows his flight instruments, like a painter knows his tubes of paint. It's something you learn.
Gentleman: And actors?
Director (casually): You give them the freedom to express themselves and try to make sure they believe in themselves. It's a simple matter. There's not much more you can do about them.
Gentleman: And time?
Director (really serious for the first time, careful and making an effort to convince the Gentleman): You see, that's made up of a host of little pieces of experience. And really, it's quite easy. You can work out plans. There are so many of them. They encircle the earth from 'time is money' in America to 'Stakhanov' in Russia. And there are people you can hire. They're tough and they keep time running to their schedules. Production directors, directors of photography, commissars, unit managers.

There's a note I have on this subject that I always keep in my wallet. May I read it to you? Even though it will take up your time?

The Gentleman nods. The Director puts his glasses on.

Director: The artist rests upon his subject. He unites with it in love. He shares the best of his spirit and his heart with it. He gives it a rebirth. In giving it birth time is of no consequence, because it is a labour of love. What lover can tell how time goes by when he is close to the one he loves? What true artist, then, is aware of time when he is working? (Pause.)

The writer of this guarantee-free confession, sir, is called Johann Wolfgang. His surname is illegible because it's been rubbed out. There you are, sir—Director of photography versus Goethe.

I looked up from the piece of paper. My financier had gone. On tiptoe. It was no loss. He was a figment of my imagination anyway.

End of the insert

Ophuls: It also offends against our job—truly and without trying to be pompous—simply against the job of serving the public—serving perhaps expresses too much inferiority—for there to be a public at all, to live with the public—this is the job it offends against, because if we want to do what people expect of us we've got to give them something which quite definitely fails to satisfy their dreams and longings, or they wouldn't keep coming to us.

Your fellow citizen, Goethe, has spoken authoritatively about this too. As usual when I'm stuck I find he's so much better at saying things for which I can't find words myself. What he said was:

Bring in Goethe quotation; M. Kehlau.

Wait for a rew words in Ophuls' voice before bringing in quotation (with Haydn music)

Kehlau: The teacher does not pay attention to his children's passing fancies, nor does the doctor to the urgent wishes and whims of his patient, nor the judge to the passions of the parties. Similarly the true artist does not regard the true object of his work as pleasing people. Like the other people I have mentioned, he tries to do as well as he can for the people he works for. But he tries to do even better for himself, and for the idea which he has conceived, for the distant goal he has set himself. He would rather that others were dragged there against their will than that he met them halfway.
Ophuls: The pursuit of success and the pursuit of finding wide appeal for a film are both enemies to it. When you're making a film you don't need to wonder whether it's going to be liked here or there or anywhere. Dürer painted very beautifully, and he never knew whether he'd be a success in New York. On the contrary—film needs failures. There is no form of artistic expression which can manage without failure, because you learn from mistakes. It's expensive if we allow ourselves mistakes in film. But that is why it's necessary—to return to the dream of the good financier—for him to have patience, whether he is a giant bank, or a lot of banks or a single bank. He must have enough patience to allow the practioners their mistakes.

The public is better than our captains of industry believe, and would have us believe. Proof of this is that without posters or publicity or any influence the public alone has decided what films shall survive. It is due to their healthy instinct alone that people still watch Garbo's or Chaplin's films or go and see this old film or that. And only if it is built upon a respect for miracles like that, which the industry must allow to continue, can I see a future for German film. In Paris I read that Ufa is buying a new site. The site will be worthless if the films go on covering old ground on the new site.

Bring in overture to The Mastersingers

Ophuls: A site does nothing. I also read in Paris, just a few days ago, a review—I'm back to music again—of a Karajan concert. The review was very sensitively written, and ended like this:

'A long time after the orchestra had risen you could see their empty golden seats. Suddenly you realised you had been involved in a great event that evening'. It is in such golden seats, through which you realise you've been involved in a great event, that the only future for German film resides. And no country is so suitable for it, no country's past has been so strong in drama and culture as Germany's. The example of Sir Laurence Olivier, whom I'm sending three telegrams to, should be the model for the German film industry.

Bring in immediately the Hamlet *monologue in English (if possible spoken by L. Olivier) as if in the distance, mixing with Ophuls'voice without stopping.*

Ophuls: In Los Angeles I saw the streets black with people who were trying to get in to see *Hamlet.* There were teenage boys who'd spent the day with bottles of Coca-Cola and, for all I know, perhaps with revolvers and beating up the road in jeeps. And they were waiting three hours each evening before they could get in and have the experience of seeing *Hamlet.* I believe emphatically that Germany is equipped for this kind of future, because it is equipped with the most important element of film, with actors. German actors look to film to become known. They want to make an impression on the world. But I believe if they copy American actors—

Bring in distant American male dialogue from an American film

—and stick their hands in their pockets, they'll only make third-rate hand-in-pocket-stickers. And I think if they were to try to match the highly-strung hypersensitivity and the absorbing,fascinating and morbid complexity of French actors—

Mix in the background French female dialogue from a French film

—they could offer us nothing more than a version of them watered down. But I am convinced that if German film is committed to German actors, and German actors are committed to their education which stretches far back behind them, which their fathers, grandfathers and everyone else have passed down to them, if they commit themselves to the classicism which they have in their bones and which could not be found so readily in any other actors in the world, they will be able to spread German film far beyond the boundaries of its own country. And the present tension, the unhealthy division between the theatre and film in Germany must cease and lead to a regeneration of the theatre and film. The relationship must be different than it is at present. My colleagues, who suffer from it, say that nowadays if they are directing at a theatre they lose their actors, who are anxious about a film contract. If they are working in film they lose their actors from the film, because actors have work to do in the theatre. It's a question of getting these things mixing together. The theatre director's box should be on wheels. The theatre director, when he has created his best production of the last two years, should leave his theatre for the studio and there transfer his best performance onto film, using the people who made it so.

I see we've long since stopped touching on problems as we travel past them, and that the 2 or the 3 or the 4—the tram I promised you—has also long since stopped. And I've stopped in front of the greatest single problem, which is insoluble and about which Thomas Mann has written:

Film is something separate from art. As crude sensation it is deeply subordinate to art and only in the most fortunate instances can it merge with art! But what is art? I don't know the answer to that. It's a position on which I stand firm. Thank you for having travelled with me this far.

Reprinted from Filmkritik. *(1956)*

Theatre, Cinema, Audience
LIEBELEI and LOLA MONTES

Frieda Grafe

It is held that there are no unacknowledged geniuses so far as film is concerned. Because of the laws of chance which regulate the showing of old films, there now exists an opportunity of revising this prejudice.

Two films have found their way back into cinema prorammes, into art house programmes at least, which have not been available to the public for years. They are two films by the same director, made almost a quarter of a century apart, which, now seen together, give proof of an admirable logical progression, of which those who attended their premieres could have had no idea.

Neither film meant much to them. *Liebelei* and *Lola Montes,* the fifth and twenty-second films of Max Ophuls, his last German films, the last before his emigration and the first after his return, which was also the last film he made. They are the best German films of a director who was regarded as French in his native land, as Austrian in France, but who came from Saarbrücken and spoke German for preference all his life long—the man whom French critics called a 'Balzacien', but who preferred to read Balzac in German.

Between *Liebelei* and *Lola Montes* there is a gap of twenty-three years and sixteen films: ten French—seven before and three after the war—and, in between, four American ones, one Italian and one Dutch. Ophuls made his last film in two versions, French and German, but with the same cast. In the one version you can hear Willy Quadflieg speaking French, in the other Martine Carol speaking German. Peter Ustinov treats both languages as foreign—that is to say, as his own.

Die Lust am Sehen (The Pleasure of Seeing) is the title of one of Ophuls' magazine articles. To quite the same extent, his films both express and demand a pleasure in hearing. For him, as the Russians say about women, it was a case of love reaching him through his ears.

He chose his main actor for *Liebelei* without having seen him. He had heard his voice over the telephone. 'He spoke clearly and simply. His voice was warm, tangible and impressive. I became a member of an audience, and could see him at the other end of the telephone'. The fact that Wolfgang Liebeneiner spoke with an unmistakably Prussian accent did not prevent Ophuls from having him play an Imperial Austrian lieutenant. And just as little with Lola Montes does an audience wonder why an Irish girl brought up in India should, of all things, speak in a French accent.

For Ophuls language was not a vehicle of predetermined content. He made it carry no messages and did not make it responsible for the past, class or character of the speaker. It is rather that his characters reveal themselves to each other and to the audience in speech in an involuntary, more than a deliberate way. 'The highest reaches of the actor's art', he wrote, 'begin, I believe, at the point where words cease to play a part . . I mean that what goes on inside a character, behind the words, is often more powerful than words themselves can be—and sometimes less powerful; that it can sometimes contradict the words, and that dialogue limps along behind emotions. I mean that experience begins long before words and continues long after words'.

Ophuls could—as Josef von Sternberg, the most closely compatible with Ophuls of any film auteur in the world, actually did—have made a film in Japanese without understanding a word of the language. In any case, the language in *Lola Montes* sounded Japanese to the film's contemporaries. 'You hear, you notice, that someone is speaking. But you are not meant to understand what is being said'. So said Friedrich Luft. He meant it in a negative sense: 'Too many experiments! Ophuls is trying to achieve too much. His basic idea falls apart in his hands'.

'There was not much speech, and you could not understand what speech there was. And if you did understand it, then the quality of the dialogue was such that it would have been better for you not to have understood it. The chief impression was of noises'. That was not written by Luft, but by Ophuls himself, not about *Lola Montes,* but about the first sound films he saw, and he meant it by no means in a negative sense. 'I saw the screen no longer as the enemy of the theatre, but as the continuation of theatre. And from that evening on I wanted to work in film'.

Ophuls sensed antagonism to theatre in film because he feared the latter's ability to subsume artistic representation into what was represented. He never deviated from this fear. As in his use of speech, so, with his increasingly sophisticated use of the moving camera, with the scenery of studio sets and properties to identify the world of film with that of reality, he fought against the blackmailing of art by reality. For him film was a spectacle, not a document of life. But never from the outset did 'the continuation of theatre'mean for him the preservation of stage plays. It meant making them dynamic.

For Ophuls the stage was no longer an autonomous artistic dream in front of an audience. Stage and stalls were seen as aspects of the same reality. They represented two perspectives which were interchangeable. Ophuls' object was to create complicity between actor and audience, at first in a playful way, later in a critical, even polemical way.

Liebelei begins at the opera. The first act of *The Abduction from the Seraglio* is over. The stage manager is looking out through the gap in the curtains into the auditorium. Perspectives are reversed. Then the great chandelier in the auditorium is switched on, as a sign that the Emperor is coming. The audience rises, turns its back on the stage and looks up at the Emperor's box, which is now the stage, while the stalls have changed their function for a second time. The visual attention of the audience in the cinema is activated by seeing the people in the stalls first as subject, then as object, then as subject again; the object being first the stage, then the auditorium, and then the Emperor's box.

The first scene of *Liebelei* is not the only example of how stage and auditorium are reversible and how this relationship continues into the cinema, into the imagination of its audience. The interchange between stage and auditorium became increasingly a stylistic device and a theme in Ophuls' films. In the final scene of *Lola Montes* the circus audience crowds in front of the cage in which Lola is on show, to lick her hand for a dollar. The camera draws back above their heads, so that for a minute the screen looks like the doorway through which the public is leaving the cinema. Here, clearly, the play with perspectives becomes a means of criticism—criticism of the public and criticism of show business.

Mizzi and Christin, the Viennese girls in *Liebelei*, snatch the opera glasses out of each other's hands so as to see the Emperor in the flesh. This is shown with sympathetic irony—but to an audience that has seen *Lola Montes* the two girls must appear related to the crowd of circus-goers. And in them the audience in the cinema must feel itself represented. The interest of the circus audience in Lola is the same as that of film fans in their stars. It is directed at the outward person, not the character, and tends to identification. The view through the opera glasses, which magnify the figure of a supreme ruler, becomes the use of the camera, which completes the process of making the audience into voyeurs.

In Ophuls' memoirs of 1946 his attitude to the audience is still at odds with itself, a product of tradition, but attacked by doubt. 'The theatre [of the Weimar Republic] did not follow the herd. The terrorism of taste by the proletariat did not take place in Germany. On the other hand I do not know whether its audience always was an audience . . . In the same way as he washed his hands before a meal, so a respectable person would go at least once a week to the theatre. In this stolid fulfilment of duty and cultural reverence he must also have swallowed and even applauded a lot of things that he really did not want to'. When, ten years later and shortly before his death, he was interviewed by François Truffaut and Jacques Rivette, he had come to to realise that: 'there is practically no such thing as an audience any more. There is a mass of consumers, that is all. They are no longer individuals, prepared to be receptive; they are just people who turn up to consume and who destroy what they want to consume'.

'I love people *en masse* as a spectacle, but not as spectators. If I had the resources I should make a film with twenty-thousand actors and show it in a tiny cinema'. Such a statement as this, which his costume designer, Georges Annenkov, recalls in his memoirs, makes one suspect Ophuls of being a supporter of a reactionary ideal of cultural elitism. But his films show the historical bankrupty of such ideals.

Ophuls' films are historical films—not because they set out to reconstruct the past (this is precisely what they do not do), but in that they mediate between historical periods. In *Lola Montes* it is not only the relationship between the present and the past of the characters that is fluid, but even the past in which Ophuls' films appear to be set is open to the present of his audience. The Vienna of *Liebelei* is not the real, past Vienna of Arthur

Schnitzler, so much as the Vienna of the present, which Ophuls first came into contact with in 1926, and of which he wrote: 'I felt as if I had not arrived in a city, but in one of Schnitzler's chapters or one of Raimund's scenes'. And the circus in *Lola Montes* certainly does not evoke the illusion of nineteenth century America. Instead, one is reminded of Wedekind, whose prologue to the *Earth Spirit* is imitated by Ustinov. In so far as theatre turns into circus it points forward to the future of show business.

The language of the theatre as a means of conveying ideas is used again here, but as heralding the language of the advertising copywriter. Linguistic anachronisms like 'star' and 'commercial' activate the audience's conception of time just as the travelling shots activate its conception of space. Ophuls' interest in making the film was aroused by reports of the fate of Judy Garland. He shows the young Lola as having an impulsive nature, whose every flash of temperament becomes a piece of successful personal publicity. She abominates advertising, sees herself as an artist, but the circus owner knows that: 'it doesn't matter a bit whether she has any talent or not. What matters is something else entirely—personality, audience-impact, and, of course, beauty'. For the late bourgeoisie, personality is not something that flourishes unseen. It goes with 'audience-impact'. And beauty does not provoke recognition, but possession. 'I know the men don't come to see her dance. They come to wait for her at the stage door'.

Ophuls encourages his audience to become aware of the present in the past, and to see that established practices had been subject to development. His critique of the present is a critique of a past that had allowed the present to come about. Even as a representative of that past, first as a stage director, then as a film author, he makes both himself and his profession the medium and the subject of his critique.

The character of the circus owner, which Peter Ustinov plays in *Lola Montes,* is at one and the same time a beautiful homage to the pioneers of show business, and an extremely accurate reckoning of accounts with them—by someone who saw himself as a man of the circus.

Die Zeit – 1968. Reprinted from E. Patalas & F. Grafe, Im Off, *Carl Hanser Verlag, Munich, 1974.*

The Bartered Bride

Frieda Grafe

A bit of Munich press coverage of 1932: 'The new form of opera film which was attempted in *The Bartered Bride* met with the wolehearted appreciation of the audience from the very beginning of the picture. Smetana's music aroused the audience's enthusiasm, and one could clearly feel the excitement rising up to the final, thunderous applause. Contrary to the pessimistic expectation that the film of the opera would produce the longueur of extended songs ... the famous ducats aria was successfully interspersed with a sequence of riding scenes ... all the Munich press ... an indigenous Munich art film well up to standard ... for Munich as a film city ... a piece of prestige ...'

I have never either heard Smetana's opera in its entirety, nor seen it staged. With Ophuls—musical direction by Theo Mackeben—all that remains of it is a sort of digest; the famous numbers which the title promises. 'Can one imagine anything worse than to hear one's favourite song in the following way: some bars of the melody and at the same time someone speaking the words, which—shoddily composed in the tradition of opera texts—are simply futile without the tune. There is really not much left of the opera, except the story and parts of music.' (A contemporary English critic in *Close Up*).

A rejection not basically dissimilar to that which Ophuls received in 1956 with *Lola Montes*—too many overlapping and contradictory voices and styles; hints of what to expect rather than the thing itself. Ophuls was supposed to have kept to the story of the opera! That is the proof you give to show that someone who has filmed a cultural work has failed to come up to his model. Smetana's basis was a libretto by Sabina. Ophuls' basis was Smetana's opera, whose music and libretto he altered. The harmony at the end and as a conclusion to the film was created in Ophuls' version by Kezal the procurer, who brings all the characters together for a family photograph. But that is a lot of people. In Smetana money ultimately finds its way back to money. The legitimate son, the first-born, marries a wife of his own standing. The avaricious procurer and the wicked stepmother, who wanted to supplant the legitimate son with her somewhat simple one, are ridiculed and driven out. Ophuls makes a tableau of it in which any idea of legitimate inheritance, logical consequence and continuity are ridiculed. His Hans is a wandering postillion, and the second-born son marries Esmeralda, the circus girl. Nor is he simple, but gentle and sensitive, and only kept silent by his mother so that love should not upset her money-making plans.

Ophuls has made the story thoroughly erotic, beautifully risqué and ambiguous. He was not primarily interested in parents who barter their children like movable property. What interested him was the bourgeois Underground*, the basis of bourgeois morality. In Ophuls' films it is forever threatened with being bankrupted by love, the unforeseeable element which destabilises wealth. Ophuls lifts the skirts of bourgeois morality (like Belmondo in *A Bout de Souffle)* finding enormous fun in the process, enjoying dreadful puns and anything regarded as vulgar. A church fair with a Try-Your-Strength machine. There is an explosion when Hans hits the button, and a trembling little marker struggling up a few centimetres when a pompous 'financial consultant' has a go. A euphemistic reading is impossible. *Dépense inproductive!***

It is only a step from the words to the idea. That step is not permissible in explicating this film. In this instance, keeping to the words is the same thing as keeping to the sounds, dwelling on the various voices which the film draws together—where everyone prevents everyone else from stealing the show. 'A major sequence in the film takes place at a fair. I travelled throughout Germany and engaged proper fairground people, who came to Geiselgasteig with their families: fire-eaters, acrobats, clowns, gypsies with their dancing bears. Fortune-tellers. (And: *Kurt Horwitz, Therese Giehse, Valentin* and *Liesl Karlstadt, Domgraf-Fassbaender, Otto Wernicke, Paul Kemp* and *Beppo Brehm* inter alia—author's note). Genuine farm boys and farm girls from the mountains.' Domgraf-Fassbaender sings a duet with Otto Wernicke, and it is not Wernicke who runs out of breath so much as Fassbaender who is deflated. The *mésalliances* and disharmonies in *The Bartered Bride* deserve attention. The destruction of bourgeois concepts of property, of the smooth and consistent circulation of wealth, is both total and subtle. These are not the amiable motives of comic opera, such as cheerful malice at the fate of the deceiver deceived. Families are ruined—mothers who are fathers, families without mothers, middle-class sons who join the circus, and middle-class daughters who go off the rails. Paralleling the selling-off of bourgeois forms of portrayal at knockdown prices there is a concerto of heterogeneous voices, cracks and gaps appear throughout the structure of portrayal and representation, in respect to which, as Ophuls shows, photography and the cinema are not innocent. The loss of the original. The mirror carried across the country road?

In a nasal accent—Baudelaire, Wedekind and Brecht rolled into one—Therese Giehse urges the public to have their photographs taken:

> Fotogrrrrrrrafiiiiiiierrrrren
> Das solle eine schöne Erinnerung für Sie sein
> Das Spiegelbild auf Papiiiiierrrr
> Das Amüsement der wirklich vornehmen Herrschaften
> In Paris, Wien, Berlin.

*In English in the original (Ed.).
**In French in the original: unproductive spending (Ed.).

Das ist nicht gemalt, das ist fotogrrrafiiiirrrt
Das ist kein Zaubermittel, das ist kein Magie
Das ist Fortschritt, das ist Wissenschaft

[Get your photogrrrrrraph
It's bound to be a beautiful souvenir
Your mirror image on paper
The pastime of the really upper-crust gentry
In Paris, Vienna, Berlin
It's not on canvas, it's a photogrrrraph
It's not magic, it isn't a conjuring trick
It's progress, it is Science]

When Giehse says *fotografieren* your ears tell you that it has something to do with writing. Scratched on to film, like McLaren. And the mirror-image on paper is flat, as flat as the fairground pictures of a hurdy-gurdy man singing of true love, and as flat as the images which break up the ducats song, when Domgraf-Fassbaender and Wernicke are hopping about on piggy-back in time to the music. The opera star as hurdy-gurdy man.

Now and then Ophuls shoots his actors at such a sharp angle from below that they look slapped on to the screen, completely two-dimensional. Here he shows how he achieves that sensation of the voluminous, which one remembers when one thinks of Ophuls' films, and how it has nothing to do with volume in reality. It comes from a flat picture and is developed by the multiplicity of voices and accents, of music, walks and gestures. By perspectives which have nothing in common with reality—windows which open like boxes, upwards. That is the impression it has made on me.

Ophuls did not like realism in the cinema, but he enjoyed the realist novelists of the nineteenth century—Stendhal, Maupassant, Balzac. *'Son âme passa dans ses oreilles et dans ses yeux. Il crut écouter par chacun de ses pores.'* (His soul flowed into his ears and his eyes. He felt he could listen through every single pore). For Ophuls realism is a literary process, not a recipe for depicting reality. That is why for him there is no such thing as a model with a claim to priority, but simply images of images. You have to look at his films with your ears because they consist of mixed forms, because they blur boundaries. He opens up networks and circles which would otherwise be static because they would insist on their isolated existences. The things he introduces into his films take on multiple values, polyvalences, which dissolve the boundaries between high and low art, and between what is mine and what is yours. The sense of freedom that you feel when you see *The Bartered Bride* (how funny it will be when everything falls apart) comes from Ophuls' lack of respect towards his source material. 'He rapes it, knocks it into shape, cuts it, leaves things out of it, pads it out, invents things, twists things and does all the other things to it that go with interpretation.' He incites you to do the same with his film. Fixating on a message would blow the light of life out of his creation. There are too many echoes, whose sources cannot be localised. Stereophonic, stereographic and stereotype:

Kezal the procurer is, in Smetana, a bad lot with a bad character. In Ophuls he is the grease that keeps the cartwheels turning. He is not driven out, as in Smetana, but, with the group photograph, he creates an ephemeral moment of harmony and peace.

And involved in this precarious moment of peace is a man who is always tripping up, lousing up the most apparently straightforward procedure or simplest statement—Valentin. 'True art unties, true art reconciles.' An endless conversation about how lovely it would be if the daughter's lover were not only rich but also had a talent for the circus. A discussion in which not a single word follows logically on the last. In the end the girl sums it up in a cliche and Valentin says that that was just what he had been trying to say. But everything that he had said had already had the effect of making commonplace expressions untrustworthy. Another scene. The circus owner's wife is supposed to lay an egg. Valentin and Karlstadt are quarrelling in front of rows of occupied seats, with their hands hiding their mouths, as it were. He hisses to her: 'Don't talk so much, or you'll stop me clucking.' As if clucking were a superior form of expression to talking! At all events it is one which corresponds exactly with Valentin's attitude to speech. For him speech is an automatic machine which produces meanings and lands you where you do not want to go. Or, put another way: clucking is the bass note, from which talking arises, becoming fixed in expressions which have little to do with the matter in hand and are nothing more than an agreement of terms for smooth-running circulation, for keeping the traffic flowing.

With Ophuls there is neither a main actor, a star, nor a theme. No single subject is allowed to parade itself as one. The main points are minor points. Digression is everything—anything to break up a subject or the impression of an exhaustive, rounded work of art. Everything is pursued with an addiction for enjoyment. Like Valentin, endlessly unfolding and poking into every cranny. The end only comes where you arbitrarily put it. And so the audience can select whom it likes to be the main character. It could be Valentin and Kezal or the circus owner and Otto Wernicke. Each of them holds an important strand of the film in his hands. One of them is busy smoothing and straightening everything out (Yes, the happiness of the country is happily in my care); the other is continually pointing out differences with his fingers until he typically, but unintentionally, sticks them in an inkwell. The village policeman says he must not forget to pay his entertainment tax, and the girl promises that she'll certainly remind her husband to forget.

Forgetting and remembering are not separate categories for Valentin. They are words which, therefore, are the things themselves, as one can tell from what the girl says. The period of time, which separates the things from the name of them, has disappeared. The question has been asked whether the form Ophuls uses is epic, like Brecht, and the similarities between the two have given rise to ideological difficulties. I would never say Ophuls was epic. The epic is too much associated with the idea of logical development through time, with one thing happening after another, while Ophuls piles things on top of each other, and creates tangles. Ophuls' films are like the way Lola's life appears. Just try to unravel in your memory the parts of Lola's life that Ustinov shows to the citizens of New Orleans, and what Ophuls shows us in the cinema and what we add to that from what we think we know about the authentic Lola. A film freely adapted from life, as the other was from Smetana.

The famous 'needle and thread' scene in *Lola Montes* is prefigured with constantly changing intonations which turn speech into song and allow it to take a rest from mere meaning. 'Roll up, Roll up, Ladies and Gentlemen', cries Liesl Karlstadt, advertising like Ustinov later does for Lola. For Ophuls, elevated language means that the sound is more audible than the words. Speech tends towards advertisement with Ophuls, not because nasty advertising has ruined pure speech but because this tendency is inherent in speech. It has always promised more than it has been able to deliver.

The space of Ophuls' films is full of holes, stitched together, a play of facets. And if these facets mirror one other thing, it is the current crisis in artistic representation, the end of the classical, realist narrative method with its author solely responsible, with its truth, its subject and with an ending which reinstates order. *The Bartered Bride* has two endings, one for the story and one for the film. Repetition, which Ophuls indulges in every possible form—and as the form most certain to produce ambivalence and ambiguity—in which he indulges at the expense of uniqueness, comes into play once more at the end. Two ends = no end. An incitement to continue, to repeat. *'Une autre chambre, un autre Stock'* (another room, another storey) as the Munich landlord says in *Lola Montes.* Life imitates books says Oscar Wilde. And if he is too frivolous a witness, then even Dante said that the passions come from books, and Lola says to Ludwig that he must do what the books expect of him.

Often by such simple means does Ophuls produce an infinity of fictions and spaces. By, for example, having Domgraf-Fassbaender with his operatic manner, movements and miming act alongside Valentin. Even to have Domgraf-Fassbaender in a film at all is like having O.E. Hasse's cultured voice coming out of Bogey's ravaged visage in a German dub. When the self-confidence of Domgraf-Fassbaender, nurtured by the artistic performance of centuries, runs into Valentin doing acrobatics without a net, there is no question of things being good enough to serve.

What I mean is this: 'When we were shooting the film I directed him (Valentin) in the way he had suggested. I explained the situation of a scene to him. For example—"Here comes the village policeman and he wants your taxes from you. You didn't pay them last year when your circus was here, and now you're afraid that if you don't pay them you'll not be allowed to put on the show. But you haven't got any money." Meanwhile the village policeman entered. Valentin called the girl over and said the first thing that came into his head. He had his own answers for every question that was put to him. When things got too complicated and had been going on too long, he clouted the village policeman on the head.'

From art to life is just a step.

Filmkritik—1970. Reprinted, with permission, from Im Off *by F. Grafe and E. Patalas, Carl Hanser Verlag, Munich, 1974.*

For an Archaeology of Lola Montes

Masao Yamaguchi

EDITORIAL NOTE: *In the following essay, the anthropologist Masao Yamaguchi argues that* Lola Montes *constitutes a layered text, a product of the encounter of a variety of texts stemming from different media. Although only the dominant discourses marked by the names of Valentin, Offenbach and Annenkov—each of them in their turn a bundle of intersecting texts—are discussed in some detail, the essay clearly demonstrates how inadequate, not to say profoundly mistaken, traditional accounts of 'influences' on a filmmaker's work can be. The point made by Mr Yamaguchi is that* Lola Montes *can be regarded as a kind of core-sample of Ophuls' work, revealing the multiple textual layers which combined to produce this particular film. Or, to change the image, that the film can be seen as an inter-textual force field holding but not in any sense unifying the various constituent discourses that compose the Ophuls text. The use of the term 'archaeology' in the title (as opposed to e.g.* Lola Montes, A Geological Survey*) stresses that this textual field should not be seen as a static, synchronous figure, but as a process of accretion and transformation spread across time, and what is more, a time which exceeds the boundaries of Ophuls' physical existence.*

The essay also provides an account from within the theoretical framework of structural anthropology of the way a figure such as Lola Montes can be produced in a place analogous to that of the 'trickster' in mythology: a figure that simultaneously marks the boundary and the articulation between two heterogeneous orders (chaos/order, inside/outside, nature/culture, and perhaps also conscious and preconscious/unconscious, semiotic/symbolic). As such, it is all the more interesting, or should one say predictable, that in patriarchal systems such a figure should be produced as female. Finally, that same anthropological perspective offers an account of the cinema as an institution which parallels the one argued by Stephen Heath, but in no way contradicts it [P. W.].

I The Encounter with Karl Valentin

In his lifetime, Ophuls encountered a great many very different people, some of them well known, others less so. In general, one could say that he derived some benefit from each encounter. However, in many cases this would be too banal a statement, as such encounters were themselves the result of his overall orientation and didn't have any transformative impact. In order to try and understand the thematic layering underpinning his work, it is necessary to try and trace the imprint of such encounters in that work, to construct a hermeneutic analogy between them.

The encounter with Karl Valentin was one such encounter that constituted a significant imprint. Not sufficient notice has been taken of Karl Valentin's collaboration with Ophuls on one of that director's earliest films: *The Bartered Bride*. The circus theme that exploded brilliantly in *Lola Montes* first emerged in the *The Bartered Bride*, made in 1932. As a logical consequence of the selection of that theme, Ophuls had this wonderful encounter with the clown in the circus, Karl Valentin. Who was Karl Valentin? This question could have been answered some ten years ago only be the readers of Martin Esslin's book on Brecht. However, today, Valentin can be appreciated in his own right, and many collections of his work have been published in Germany and in France over the past five years, as readers of the *Times Literary Supplement* have been able to learn from the reviews.

In the interview with François Truffaut and Jacques Rivette reprinted in this book (p.16), Ophuls talked about Karl Valentin with great affection and admiration, although without mentioning his name. But as the interviewers weren't interested in Ophuls' marvellous memory of Valentin, they changed the topic, alas! Valentin was a genuine incarnation of the spirit of spectacle, although one could also define him as a cabaret poet, in the tradition represented today by Wolf Biermann. He was Brecht's teacher of the streets. It was through him that Brecht learnt the actual technique of *Verfremdung* (distantiation). Valentin didn't just perform the role of a clown in Ophuls' film, he really was a clown on the cabaret stage as well as in the circus. Therefore, for Brecht, Valentin's disciple, distantiation was not merely a separate, abstract technique derived from serious theatre but it was related to the tradition of the clown in the popular entertainment area. We do not know whether Ophuls ever came across Brecht or not. But he nevertheless did encounter him through the mediation of Valentin. Today we know that Ophuls shares many features with Brecht and that they have many aesthetic techniques in common. One example is the recourse to the narrator derived from the traditions of popular entertainment as a distantiation agent, such as the singer of the moritat in the *Threepenny Opera* and in *The Bartered Bride*, the ringmaster in *Lola Montes* and the *meneur de jeu* in *La Ronde*. Although one could point to the possible influence of Wedekind's play *Earth Spirit* and *Pandora's Box* with their ringmaster figure, still the idea of the significance of clowning was a constant presence in both Brecht's and Ophuls' mind. As a matter of fact, the clown and the circus never ceased to fascinate Ophuls, as can be seen from an anecdote remembered by George Annenkov, who reports Ophuls as saying: 'Clown-animals . . . why not? We are dealing with symbols, and there are so many pigs amongst men, so many asses too . . . And clown-objects? Just think of the decisive role sometimes played by objects in human life!'

The polysemic aspect of words and images enables us to play on the potential signification of these terms as manifested in relation to clowns because of their ambiguous existence as floating signs, bridging diverse areas of meaning. To the masters of paradox and irony, our rigid classificatory distinctions between man and animal, animate and inanimate, man and object, do not matter. By referring to an inanimate object, they draw attention to the inanimate aspect of human beings. They are the apostles of multiple expression. From reading Valentin's texts or listening to his songs and words (e.g. on the Telefunken record entitled *Chanson and Cabaret in Berlin in the Twenties,*), one can say that without a doubt this minor actor in *The Bartered Bride* left as big a mark in Ophuls' world of filmic imagery as he did in Brecht's work.

II The Encounter with George Annenkov

It would appear that the collaboration with George Annenkov, stage and costume designer of a number of Ophuls' films, including *Lola Montes,* was the outcome of one of Ophuls' most propitious encounters. Annenkov, an emigre artist from Russia, was in the best position to understand Ophuls' artistic background. He knew the artistic milieu of the 20th century well. In his book on Ophuls, Annenkov gave an excellent description of their encounter. He had seen *Liebelei* in Paris in 1933 after he'd left Russia, but they only met in 1950 when Ophuls asked him to do the costume designs for *La Ronde.* Both men already were familiar with each other's work. While they were talking about Schnitzler, Annenkov told him about Vsevolod Meyerhold as one of the greatest stage directors of the century, someone who regarded traditions of popular entertainment, circus spectacle and *commedia dell' arte* as crucial models for the theatrical form. Annenkov had devoted a somewhat lengthy chapter to Meyerhold in his book *Unforgettable People,* praising the staging of Alexander Blok's play *Fairground Booth* as one of the most radical of the twentieth century theatre. Because Meyerhold's notion of biomechanics was misunderstood and became a mere label, he came to be regarded as the promulgator of abstract theatre. In fact, today his theatre might more accurately be described as semiotic theatre, in which the formal concerns were deeply embedded in what he had learnt from the world of circus and *commedia dell' arte.* Meyerhold's interests in these forms of representation made a powerful impact on for instance the work of Eisenstein, his one-time disciple, who also professed a great interest in such popular forms of spectacle. It is well known that Eisenstein's technique of typage finds its roots in those forms of theatrical representation.

Similarly, in that both refer back to the same forms of spectacle and theatre, Eisenstein's notion of montage of attractions and the fragmentation of the spectacular form in *La Ronde* and *Lola Montes* are not unrelated. Both constitute possible strategies for de-familiarisation effects (*Verfremdung*). In this context, and in the light of the fact that Annenkov, when he first met Ophuls, talked at some length about Meyerhold's ideas and his staging of Schnitzler's *The Veil of Pierrette*, the description of this event in Edward Braun's book *Meyerhold on Theatre* (1969) is worth quoting: 'Freely adapted by himself (Meyerhold) the work bore scant resemblance to the original, and even the title was altered to *Columbine's Scarf*. The aim was to banish the cloying sweetness often associated with pantomine and create a chilling grotesque in the manner of E.T.A. Hoffmann. The three scenes were broken down into fourteen fleeting episodes, in order that the spectator should be shocked by the constant switches of mood into an unquestioning acceptance of the play's own ghastly logic.'

This kind of shock effect, which in fact precisely questions the play's ghastly logic rather than forcing an unquestioning acceptance, was also implicit in the strategy of intertwining the two narrative patterns in *Lola Montes:* one presented as a series of flash backs on the life story of Lola, the other set in the circus as seen through the mediation of the ringmaster.

Annenkov and Ophuls also talked about Alexander Tairov, another Russian stage director who belonged to the group that introduced elements of spectacle via the *commedia dell' arte* and Hoffmann into the theatre. Indeed, it is no accident that Offenbach, so adored by Ophuls, also transformed Hoffmann's tales into an opera. There is in fact a long line of film directors, composers, stage directors and playwrights whose work is grounded in the traditions of spectacle, generating the use of devices such as the merry-go-round form evidenced in *La Ronde.* To name but a few: Hoffmann, Mozart, Offenbach, Schnitzler, Alexander Blok, Wedekind, Nikolai Evreinov, Meyerhold, Tairov, Eisenstein, Annenkov, Vakhtangov, Max Reinhardt, etc. Ophuls links into this current and appears to have been one of the last to combine this long and venerable tradition with avant garde experimentation producing a specific mode of representation straddling popular spectacle and avant garde practices. It is in that context that we can argue with A. Williams (for details see the *Familmographic Romance* in this book) when he states that 'the very notion of representation is a major subject of *Lola Montes*'. All forms of aesthetic representations of reality are depicted in the film, from dance to music, from opera to theatre, from shadow plays to painting, etc. In each case, it is precisely the very notion of any literal rendering of reality that is mocked. In relation to *Lola Montes,* it is not only Offenbach's operatic practices which functioned as models. Wedekind's play *Lulu* almost certainly provided one of the models for the construction of the film's tissue of images and sounds. Annenkov reports that he told Ophuls about Fedor Kommisar—zhevsky's staging of *Lulu* in Moscow in 1918. And when Annenkov sited such examples of his conception of theatre, Ophuls replied: 'That's perfect. We have found our common language.' This was indeed the case, and their common language was best spoken in the circus arenas to which Annenkov had been committed in his Russian work and which he was pleased to be able to revive in the decors and costume design of *Lola Montes.* In this way, the film can be seen as a space articulating the concerns of the Russian avant garde (and of the twenties movements in general) and the post-war European cinema.

That Ophuls was more than ready to perform such a function is amply illustrated by his remark to Annenkov: 'In my film, the circus assumes precisely a symbolic sense. If I put giants next to lilliputians, that is to show that life contains extemes: there is beauty, but there is also revulsion; there is happiness and suffering *und so weiter*... Although I may insist on a dominant colour for a particular episode, I want all colours to collide with each other in the arena of the circus, because my circus runs through an entire life, encompassing all its stages...' When he used the phrase 'symbolic sense' it almost reads as 'cosmic sense'. Ophuls appears to have been aware of the nature of circus as the space of encounter between nature/culture, periphery/centre, inside/outside as defined by present-day semioticians of culture.

It is against this background that the filmic space of *Lola Montes* was constructed as a space which allowed for the inscription of cosmic contradictions rather than for the depiction of a heroine's life story or as the scene for the development of a linear narrative. The importance of this fact was underlined by Annenkov when he wrote: 'But through and beyond his (Ophuls) laughter, his words, his pacing up and down, his sudden stops, the circus, the circus of Max Ophuls and that of Lola Montes, began to take shape, to develop, to materialise all by itself.' Annenkov wasn't at all surprised to witness the process of transformation of people and objects into caricatures in Ophuls' circus: 'It is a myth, a whirling allegory.'

As a rule, we do not hesitate to talk of myth in relation to e.g., Visconti's work, but we are not used to referring to Ophuls' work as mythical. One reason is perhaps that the current notion of myth still stems from the Wagnerian model. However, there is another understanding of myth as a form that mediates, articulates two polar opposites by means of, say, laughter, acrobatics, jokes, clowning, inversions, etc. This is the kind of myth upon which Ophuls' work is founded. Mikhail Bakhtin, in his seminal works on Rabelais and Dostoyevsky, forged the concept of the carnivalesque to refer to the type of language involved in the representation of such myths. There is no doubting that circus constitutes a symbolic and carnivalesque space where oppositions such as high/low, beautiful/ugly, bright/obscure, centre/periphery, tragic/comic can be articulated. Similarly, *Lola Montes* constitutes such a device for the articulation of these oppositions through the deployment of filmic sounds and images. It is in this sense that the construction of narrative space as an ambiguous space was at times more important to Ophuls than the hero or heroine of the story itself. This emerges in Ophuls' account of his intentions as noted down by Annenkov: 'Lola is merely an axis around which the drama unfolds..., that is not to say that in this way I want to minimise

Lola's role. Only that in the film, I am displacing the centre of gravity. Lola must be a perfect comedienne, because she is the one who provokes the dramas that interest us, she is their trigger.' As *agent provocateur* belonging outside the structure of the everyday world, thus symbolically located in a position that mirrors that of the cinema itself as a medium, Lola is transformed by her very existence in that place into a mythical figure, displacing the characters surrounding her, taking them out of the well defined roles of ordered everyday life into the space of the carnival where everything can be mixed together and turned into its opposite. One of the 19th century forerunners of this notion of the spectacular, the carnivalesque, was Offenbach, to whom Ophuls was so profoundly attached throughout his life.

III The Encounter with Offenbach

One of the keys to an understanding of the founding themes of Ophuls' work, and one that usually escapes the attention of the critics, is Ophuls' devotion to the work of Offenbach. This oversight can readily be explained in view of the current music and theatre milieu's lack of interest in that composer. Nowadays, it is difficult to comprehend why someone as prestigious as Siegfried Kracauer, author of *From Caligari to Hitler,* published in the late thirties a book entitled *Jacques Offenbach and the Paris of his Age.* Ophuls' interest in opera and in the operatic work of Mozart is well documented (see for instance his long standing project to film *Don Juan*), but it is the work of Offenbach he put forward as a model for the creation of a specifically European musical film genre as opposed to and on a par with the great American tradition of musicals epitomised by the work of Vincente Minnelli at MGM. When asked which works might provide the basis for a European musical, Ophuls replied: 'With any Offenbach. That really is the music of my life. 'When his questioner objected and pointed out that Offenbach wasn't even French, Ophuls commented: Isn't that monstrous! Although one could read this anecdote as an illustration of Ophuls' angry reaction at the implied slur on his and Offenbach's jewishness, that is less important in this context than that he proclaimed Offenbach's work to be the music of his life. At one time, he confessed to Annenkov rather enviously: 'You have made Goethe's *Faust* and Offenbach's *La Belle Hélène.* You even did all of Offenbach's work! Me, I can't manage that yet.' Annenkov apologised, pointing out that he didn't stage Goethe's *Faust* but the one by Gounod. Nevertheless, Ophuls often remarked on his fascination for Murnau's *Faust* and with the whole of Goethe's work. But why then was he so attached to Offenbach's music? What could he have seen in it? One reason is probalby that Offenbach was undoubtedly the musican most directly and intimately concerned with the world of spectacle as evidenced in his *Tales of Hoffmann.* He also had a great sense of humour and a taste for parody, his stage at times brimming over with the spirit of the clown, a feature possibly derived from the *commedia dell' arte,* as can be seen in his *Bluebeard.* Popular tunes, carefree and cheerful musicality, wit, the detachment generated by the absurd, a charm that doesn't lose its critical bite, bold utilisation of scenic space in the style of popular entertainments, these are the elements Ophuls appears to have found in Offenbach and which in many ways dovetailed with his own conception of spectacle, as amply illustrated by the structure and *mise en scene* of *Lola Montes*.

This love of Offenbach explains to some extent why Ophuls agreed to take the trite story of Lola Montes, a cheap and vulgar novel, as the basis for a filmscript. Two factors appear to have been involved. One was that he wasn't offered an alternative, the other that he felt sorely tempted to refuse on the grounds that he didn't like the story of a heroine in whose life there were far too many events. He nevertheless accepted. And he transformed Lola from the conventional notion of the heroine into a figure—as opposed to a character—around which other figures turn, rather like the merry-go-round that functions as the pivot of *La Ronde*. At this point, I would like to put forward a hypothesis, fully cognisant of its status as conjecture, although by no means offered as 'idle' speculation: there are many reasons providing sufficient grounds for the hypothesis to be substantiated as a result of more intensive analyses. I would suggest that Ophuls agreed to do *Lola Montes* because of the similarity of the story to Offenbach's *La Pèricole*. Both are related to Latin America (Mexico and Peru respectively), both deal with impossible relationships between a woman of the people and a member of the nobility, a fairly common situation that can easily be transformed into absurdity, and both have a provocative woman, a trickster to use the anthropological term, as the heroine at the centre of the plot. The possibility of a cheap story being turned into a fairground booth absurdity must have attracted Ophuls, as it might have Offenbach.

In respect of his interest in the combination of popular spectacle with traditions of classic 'high art', Ophuls isn't so far removed from Jean Renoir, with whom he is often linked. For instance, Offenbach's *La Pèricole* and Ophuls' *Lola Montes* share a great many features with Renoir's *The Golden Coach*, including the reference to Prosper Merimèe, which underpins both Renoir's and Offenbach's work and crosses Ophuls' path directly, though unhappily, in the form of *Colomba*, the basis for the film *Vendetta* Ophuls was to make in Hollywood. In these stories, it is the ambiguity of women from the world of popular entertainment that provides the source of the dramatic development. It would appear then that it is under the spell of Offenbach that Ophuls finally agreed to go ahead and film this penny dreadful about Lola Montes. As such, his interest can safely be described as being produced by, held in a chain of interlinking texts, an inter-textual field.

Finally, in relation to the theme of the woman as transgressor emerging from the world of popular entertainment, it would be difficult to ignore the parallels that exist between Lola and Lulu, Frank Wedekind's creation. In a review that can be read as malicious, John Simon wrote of *Lola Montes:* 'The life story of the notorious dance-courtesan is told in terms of an extended circus metaphor—a ringmaster is putting on a spectacular circus show, whose tableaux are jumping-off points for flashbacks; cracking his whip, he describes

Lola as the most dangerous wild beast of all, and, at the end of the film, exhibits her in a cage. This idea, the best in the film, is a steal from Frank Wedekind's *Earth Spirit*, in whose prologue a similarly bedizened and whip-wielding animal trainer steps before the curtain and introduces the heroine, Lulu, as a snake that can embrace a tiger to death.' (*Movie into Film*, New York 1971, p 353). For the purposes of the review, this critic tactfully forgot that Wedekind borrowed the plot of *Earth Spirit* form the text of a circus pantomine called *Lulu* written by the now long forgotten Felician Champsaur in 1893. the heroine of the story was the charming and transgressive *femme fatale* represented in the circus by the figure of Columbine. Wedekind appears to have been inspired by this spectacle during his stay in Paris working as scriptwriter for a German circus. The point here is not so much one of direct 'influence', but rather that their work was a natural outcome of both authors' interest in the circus.

In relation to a knowledge of the milieu that supplied the authors with the model of the space on which they built these dramatic structures, the use of, say, a ringmaster is of secondary importance. The main aspect of these works is that they are self-reflexive, that they are about the very medium in which they find expression. Except for the well patronised theatre, most popular theatre and cinema were located in the obscure spaces that exist within an urban milieu, at times closely connected with fairgrounds and market places, where vice was more directly manifested than in the peaceful residential quarters. The majority of popular entertainment, including the circus, drew its driving force from the exploration of horror and other strong sensations or sinister feelings people associate with that kind of 'intermediate' space. A type of space that also inspired for instance, the German expressionist theatre and cinema. While Wedekind was regarded as a precursor of that expressionist theatre, Ophuls at times described himself as a product of expressionist cinema.

The *femme fatale* was nothing but the mediator, the point of articulation between the *Earth Spirit* and the audience's expectation of a confrontation with such a being. We may well venture the assertion that such *femme fatales* represent the transgression of nature into the well ordered territory of culture through the mediation of the *geni loci* called fairground booths or cinemas, their twentieth century version. This explains why these authors preferred to take their heroines from the world of popular entertainment. They constituted a most suitable spiritual medium for the transformation, through the activation of desire to see and scrutinze, of the audience's wish to escape the boring, set and coded patterns of everyday life. Some of these transgressors are presented in the comic mode (e.g. Champsaur's *Ur-Lulu*, *La Péricole*, Hoffmann's *Princess Brambilla*—staged by Tairov), others in the tragic mode (e.g. Wedekind's *Lulu* and Ophuls' *Lola Montes*), yet others in the absurd or ambiguous mode (e.g. most of Offenbach's *opera bouffe* heroines and Gozzi-Vakhtangov's *Princess Turandot*), but all of these figures allowed the production of a sharp contrast between life (eros) and death (thanatos), the theme of the 'dark lady' being related to the ambiguous status of the theatrical space itself (whether it be fairground booth, circus or cinema) through the negativity, the danger they represent for the coded everyday order of the well tamed citizen's life. These heroines' brilliant costumes, far in excess of the customary canons of modesty, are glorified and balanced by their precarious position in theatrical space, located as they are on the side of total negativity. Spectacle in the form best suited for the representation of a world in its totalilty, because it allows the articulation (reconciliation?) between chaos and order, absurdity and sobriety, death and life, (indeed, death into life), clowning and seriousness, fantasy with realism, myth with history, periphery and centre. Spectacle achieves this by allowing these opposites, at the very least, to co-exist, successfully or not. In this sense, the notion of *Lola Montes* as a meta-spectacle, as Alan Williams puts it, can be seen as one of the forms which the avant gardes of the first half of this century led up to, occupying a terrain that comprises Fellini's grotesques, Eisenstein's notion of montage, Brecht's concept of epic theatre, Artaud's aspiration towards theatre as epidemic, Visconti's attempt to present history in the form of an operatic spectacle, and so on. It is this kind of practice generated during the first half of the century, that might survive the second half.

The Ophuls Text: A Thesis.

Paul Willemen

The few reviewers and critics that have attempted to deal with Ophuls' films all revert regular as clockwork to a handful of terms such as baroque, style, camera virtuosity, rhythm, formalist, fascination, romantic, nihilist, etc. As Alan Williams pointed out in his thesis on Ophuls[1], the traditional film theories have been unable to cope with the work of Ophuls: starting with the idea that he must be an author as opposed to a mere director, his work is then reduced to empty formalisms or 'pure style', praised by the so-called *mis en scène* critics such as Jacques Rivette, or dismissed by moralists fixated on forms of content such as 'characters' and themes. Accepting this crude form/content opposition, a few others sought for profound statements about the human condition in selected combinations of 'style' and 'story'. The most productive and intelligent approaches have concentrated on the specific combinations in Ophuls' work of the sequence-shot and montage (Brian Henderson, Victor Perkins and Andrew Sarris), thus to some extent demonstrating why neither montage critics nor sequence-shot critics such as André Bazin were able to find a way of reading the peculiar 'in between' strategies deployed in the films.

A second set of terms that surfaces regularly in writing about Ophuls is that his films all focus on women, even if the original source material for the plot, no matter how classic or prestigious a piece of literature it may be, has to be pulled rather violently in that direction. The best examples are perhaps *Liebelei* and *Werther*, where in each case a female character somehow gets to be dramatically privileged over the male protagonist. This notion relates, as will be argued later, to the fact that in these films, as in the rest of Ophuls' work, women tend to be produced as pivots within intricate and elaborate narrative structures and as privileged objects of the look, that of the audience as well as that of intra-diegetic characters.

A third set of terms, produced mainly by content oriented critics, relates to a contradiction between the filmed and the filming. For instance, Karel Reisz remarked in an essay in *Sequence* (No. 14, 1952): 'Ophuls is clearly fascinated by the world he depicts, but never allows its surface charm to obscure the price that has to be paid for its preservation. The social conventions, so pleasant to observe from a distance, conceal a rigid and merciless discipline.'

This rigidity, this rigorous Order, transgression of which can bring death, is then depicted in the most fluid and flexible of ways. As if what was repressed by the Law, the rigorous social order, re-emerges as excess in the *mise en scène*. The most striking example here is perhaps the literalism, i.e. the literal production in the filmic text of a verbal metaphor in *Le Plaisir*. As a joke, and it is interesting that he should have chosen to say it in this way, Ophuls explained that the reason for the convoluted crane movement along the walls of the brothel in the *Maison Tellier* episode, peering through windows but never cutting to the inside of the house, was because the Maison Tellier was precisely a *maison close*, a closed house. Behind its doors and windows is locked away what a rigorous social morality excludes from its legal order. So the camera is on the side of the Law, but it is the repressed (here the repression of the verbal term combined with the inscription of socio-sexual repression) which moves it along, obsessively circling its object of fascination, describing in its movement the outlines of the gaps in the social fabric, catching glimpses of the forbidden areas, but from the outside. The tracks, dollys and crane movements constantly holding out the promise that in passing, or in the shift from one look to another as, e.g., in the transition via the spyglass in *The Exile*, the look may find its object of desire. But never shall it be offered too detailed and close up a scrutiny by a fixed gaze. It is also interesting to note that Ophuls appeared to be aware of the sexual implications of isolating a person for the look, the sexual implications of cutting to close-ups offering, e.g., the body of a woman for access to the look. In *Le Plaisir,* he shoots the five prostitutes in the train in mid- and long-shots, always attempting to keep as many of them as possible in frame at the same time. The reason for this, Ophuls explained, referring to another literalism, was that Maupassant described the women as 'a bunch of flowers' and that he was reluctant to 'pick' one of them! The film that turns entirely on this inscription of the look and the desired scene is of course *Lola Montes,* where the woman is explicitly and directly put on show, offered to the fixed and fixing gaze of viewer (in the film and of the film) and camera. But what the look finds is a mask, the woman as masquerade, as screen. The film's narrative and diegesis fragment under the pressure of the desire of penetrating beyond that mask, with the look as mark of desire to possess what always escapes. Every new scene/seen promising to satisfy what the previous one provoked. But as the 'real' object is never that which the look finds, always landing on a stand-in, the look is offered (moves to) scene after scene, each constituting a trap for it, something in which it can loose itself, something to 'fill' the eye and capture it, but nevertheless always lacking what it is looking for, and thus forever re-launching the wish to look again or to look elsewhere. It is in this sense that Ophuls' films engage with the cinema as spectacle, or, to put it in the words of Stephen Heath, 'with the relations sustained in cinema, as cinema'. In Ophuls, cinema becomes a machine for the entrapment of the look. It is also in this sense that the function of the soundtrack of the films can begin to be understood: the inscription of signifiers off screen, emphasising the unseen, what has been withheld from the eye. Alan Williams remarked[2] that often the soundtrack refers to represented spectacles such as theatre or opera performances, i.e. precisely what is socially given to and for the look, while the cinema thus comes to stand under the sign of the look at that which is socially withheld, reactivating as an institution specifically designed for this, the nexus look/desire and scene/seen. According to the rules of patriarchy, it is at this intersection that the figure of woman is produced as image. At the juncture of order, the Law and the repressed, the unconscious, woman is produced as the signifier of desire. Moreover, a signifier which represents the subject for that other signifier, the look, thus instituting and producing the cinema spectator, that specific subject produced by/for the cinematic institution.

The ceaseless metonymy set in motion by the look, the ceaseless inscription of difference (the scene is never quite what is to be seen), in order for the film to remain within a certain formula of narrative, indeed for it to end at all, it must be circumscribed, contained in some way. Interestingly, for a cinematic practice turning on the look, a number of the films end by the inscription of a full stop on the sound track (see, e.g. *Liebelei, Letter From An Unknown Woman, Madame de...*): the duel marked by the pistol shot (or expected shot) off screen, present only as sound, in the same way that the social spectacles referred to above are marked as sounds only. In the duel scenes, it is the sound that ends the film, not the image track which often spills over into an epilogue extendable at infinitum, signifying not so much a coming to rest as a freezing of a particular scene, as with the couple on the beach, one in an invalid's chair, frozen as a specific relationship for the rest of their lives and gradually letting the image track run out. It isn't that there is no more to be seen, merely that, from then on, everything is endless repetition or rather: sameness, marked by the signifier of total loss, death. What the sound track puts an end to is the difference, the desire which drove the look from one stand-in to another, by as it were filling with a sound that gap between what was looked for and what was available to be looked at. It isn't surprising that such a sound should simultaneously signify death.

The dialectic of order and excess turning on the pivot of the look at the female also finds its mark on three different levels in the films, one related to the narrative structure, the other two to the *mise en scène.* Firstly, as suggested earlier, the impact of the scopic drive on the narrative fragments and distorts it. The linear, orderly telling of the story from beginning to end breaks open, turns back on itself, regresses (flashes back) on the trace of the memory of plentitude. The expectation of the look satisfied produces a movement backwards into the future, the expected recovery in the future (of the unreeling of the film, scene after scene) of the memory of the look satisfied. A variant on this: the perpetual re-commencing of the story, the renewal of the trajectory, the repetition or doubling of scenes (see, e.g. *La Ronde, Le Plaisir, La Tendre Ennemie* for the recommencing of stories, while *La Ronde, Madame de...* and *Letter From An Unknown Woman* offer startling examples of doubled scenes). Once more the complex inscription of this aspect of the dialectic is to be found, not surprisingly, in the very same film that most directly and explicitly engages with the cinematic representation of the look: *Lola Montes.*

Secondly, the dialectic of balance, symmetry on the one hand and excess on the other, is also to be found on the level of the arrangement of the pro-filmic event: characters will be placed in symmetric or harmoniously balanced relations to each other, with figures on the left/right of the screen, or objects balancing a figure on the other side of the frame, or threesomes with the side figures looking at the central one, etc. Even the sets reproduce this sense of symmetry via double stairways, the shape of a circus tent, the entrance to a house, mirrors reflecting a figure, etc. Simultaneously, however, there is a proliferation of excessive detail, filling up the image with impediments to the look, obstacles between scene and seen, as well as the proliferation of objects in the sets themselves, literally filling the image to overflowing, offering an endless series of objects for the gaze. In this sense, the look is invited to wander through the scene resting now on one object, then on another, while on the other hand the overall composition offers the spectacle of fixed proportions harmoniously balanced in the most classical manner, guiding and captivating the look, directing it to the focus of the frame. The result is that the look is simultaneously subjected to two forces, pulling it in different directions.

Thirdly, there is the conduct of the camera: the combination of restlessness, ceaseless movement, the function of which was indicated earlier, with repetitions of movements at different times, although often accompanying a doubled scene on the level of the narrative, as, e.g., the movements and camera positions in the station and church scenes in *Madame de...* (a film in which nearly every element is doubled, replayed, echoed or inverted, either simultaneously via mirrors or at a later moment in the film) and the repeated tracking shots in *Letter From An Unknown Woman.* A second aspect of the camerawork in relation to the pro-filmic event reproducing the stasis/process dialectic, to use Julia Kristeva's terminology, is the use of a moving camera in relation to a moving figure, both remaining equidistant and thus in a fixed, static relation to each other, while the process, the excess is displaced onto the background objects (furniture, walls, trees, etc) moving through the image. The clearest example of this occurs towards the beginning of *Madame de...* where she moves through her appartment at a frantic pace but at a fixed distance from the camera accompanying her movements, the furniture and decors providing the movement in the frame, in a way echoing the revolving landscapes in the amusement park in *Letter From An Unknown Woman.*

Each of these registers of text construction inscribes simultaneously a breakthrough of excess, the transgression of a 'rigid and merciless discipline' as Karel Reisz put it, and the strategies to contain and recover, to neutralise through re-inscription or repetition what the Law had to expell, to repress in order for it to come into existence. In that sense, Ophuls' cinema can be seen as the dramatisation of repression, where the repressed returns and imprints its mark on the representation, undermining and at times overwhelming that manifestation of secondary elaboration called 'a coherent scenario'.

Notes

[1] Alan Williams wrote: 'Roy Armes, in a formulation which is representative of those critics who dismiss Ophuls, has called the director "... virtually a test case of one's approach to the cinema. For those whose concern is purely visual and whose ideal is an abstract symphony of images, Ophuls has the status of one of the very great directors. For spectators and critics who demand in addition to the images the sort of human insight and moral depth that a play or a novel can give, he is merely a minor master, a maker of exquisite but rather empty films." *(The French Cinema since 1946, Vol.I.)*

An entire monograph could be written examining the critical presuppositions which structure these few sentences. We would wholeheartedly agree that Ophuls is a 'test case' of thinking about film, but the 'test' is not demonstrated with the *help* of the style/content dichotomy invoked here, but by the very *fact* that the dichotomy arises at all. Here, in a particularly superficial case, style equals image and content equals 'human insight and moral depth'. These two are taken, implicitly, as wholely independent. (. . .) The subjects of many Ophuls films are pretexts for the films themselves as spectacles in tneir own right. 'Content analysis' is not appropriate, for the films are not 'about' their subjects in any direct manner (and, furthermore, these subjects are borrowed from other works). For this reason, the present study has eschewed filmic 'content' except as it is inflected by modes of presentation. A 'subject' summary by Richard Roud (in *Max Ophuls — An Index)* demonstrates the problems of content analysis as applied to Ophuls: "What are Ophuls' subjects? The simplest answer is: women. More specifically: women in love. Most often, women who are unhappily in love, or to whom love brings misfortune of one kind or another. The surroundings in which they live are usually luxurious, in any event, they generally manage at least one performance at the opera and one ball during the course of the film. They usually live between 1880-1900. . . . The setting is usually 'Vienna': sometimes it is actually Vienna. Either way it is not the real *finde-siècle* Vienna but rather an ideal Vienna—the city of operetta and Strauss waltzes."

This passage exempliifies one of the most typical strategies of contemporary film criticism as applied to directors—the attempt to construct an 'ideal film,' of which the actual works are mere manifestations. (. . .) The problem is that Sarris and the other auteurists merely changed the emphasis of the *politique des auteurs* without discarding (in practice, if not in theory) two of its more suspect premises. First, the notion of an all-powerful and consistent creative force is still invoked to valorise minor films of favoured directors at the expense of notable works by otherwise undistinguished ones. (. . .) The auteurists' second, more damaging premise is the implicit retention of the notion of an 'ideal film' only imperfectly expressed in an *auteur's* actual works. *Madame de*. . . and *Letter From An Unknown Woman* are the auteurists' favoured Ophuls films; they are also the most 'typical', in terms of their subjects (they share all of the features cited by Roud, above). *Auteur* criticism does not seem interested in *La Ronde*, for example, except in that it relates to these two films.' A.L. Williams, *Max Ophuls and the Cinema of Desire—Style and Spectacle in Four Films, 1948-1955, Univ. of New York at Buffalo, 1977 (unpublished).*

[2] In each case, the apparent contradiction between interpolated representation (opera) and narrative (the supposed lived experience of the characters) results from a temporarily restricted spectator knowledge of the latter. *Letter From An Unknown Woman*, *Madame de*. . ., and *Lola Montes* all share the curious trait of never actually showing the spectator the performance that is heard. In each case, visual information remains within the narrative universe while aural information (the arias, the sound of Lola's feet on the stage) refers to the performance. In this way the spectator is required to actively integrate (perceive simultaneously) levels of the filmic universe which are, for the purposes of understanding, resolutely separate . . . Again, the final result of this structure is not to suggest that 'art falsifies life', even though this reading is suggested at particular points. Rather, it is the relation of 'life' to the spectacle which is called into question. The societies and characters presented in the films are themselves suggested to be works of representation. In this context, the opera, theatre, and dance performances strewn through the films are representations of representations.' Alan Williams, *op. cit.*

The Question Oshima

Stephen Heath

Reactions and commentaries so far have made it only symptomatically clear that the force of *Empire of the Senses (Ai no corrida*—Oshima Nagisa, 1976) is that of a question decisively posed to the cinema (and thus to any 'new' European or American cinema); a film which today remains untouched by that force will not be contemporary but ideologically reactionary. The question lies in the articulation of the sexual, the political, and the cinematic, and in the impossibilities discovered in the process of such an articulation (hence, indeed, the reactions and commentaries, themselves entirely and predictably possible: the reassertion, by defenders as well as critics, of the grounds of the expected, of 'what can be taken'). Briefly, the following notes work out from the problem of the cinematic institution—'the imaginary signifier'—in an attempt to refind something of the impossible of Oshima's film, of its experience of limits, to demonstrate the effective terms of its question, more important than the film itself, or, rather, the very point of its importance.

Consider a film such as *Letter From An Unknown Woman* (Max Ophuls, 1948), a film of which from one perspective—that of the question to cinema—*Empire of the Senses* is the direct and ruinous remake. At the centre of *Letter From,* a classic Hollywood narrative film with genre specificities (the 'woman's film') and stylistic markings ('Ophuls' as the name for 'extensive use of music, long elaborate takes with flowing camera movements', etc.), is the full image, sexuality as look, the *looked-for-image.* Lisa (Joan Fontaine) models and is *the model:* radiantly dressed and lit, she circles for the gaze of prospective clients at the fashionable dress-shop where she earns her living and at the same time for that of the spectator who has paid to *see* the film; twice, as she does so, men, spectators in the film, respond to the perfection of the flawless—*whole*—body, to the image of a female beauty, of the female *as beauty,* which holds the sexual cinematically as just that: the desired and untouchable image, an endless *vision.* As always, however, the centred image mirrors a structure that is in excess of its effect of containment, that bears the traces of the heterogeneity—the trouble—it is produced to contain: sexuality here is also the 'more' that the look elides, that is elided from the look and that returns, constantly, in the figures of its absence. After the first modelling scenes, Lisa spends one night with Stefan (Louis Jourdan), the man she has loved and worshipped in silence since childhood; as they begin to kiss, the image fades, the screen is left black with nothing to see. Evidently, this is convention, its context the Hays Code, the awareness of what can and cannot be shown. But convention is never simply a fact outside a film: what can and cannot be shown, the determining confines of image and look, is there in *Letter From,* is part of its film action and meaning. The fade, the image absent, is *Letter From's* momentary and fundamental figure, comprising in its elision the time of acknowledgment and consequent guilt (Lisa is caught up in the more than the image, the one night makes her pregnant, detailing her suffering the film details her punishment for transgression) *and* of denial and consequent innocence (the unshown leaves Lisa pure, intact as image, still perfect; she is only ever daughter or sister and then mother to Stefan, never—the exact function of the fade, the meaning of the convention in the film—a sexual lover). Immediately afterwards, the film goes back to the image of Lisa modelling, now for Stefan, and continues with its drama of vision, the image that Stefan has lost and the images that he remembers as Lisa remembers in her letter, as we remember through the narrative which orders our memory of the film, *our* vision.

Centred image, drama of vision, space of the look, towards a coherence of vision for us: classically, narrative cinema operates on a very powerful apparatus of 'looks' which join, cross through, and relay one another. Thus: (1) the camera looks (a metaphor assumed by this cinema) . . . at someone, something: the profilmic; (2) the spectator looks . . . at, or on, the film; (3) each of the characters in the film looks . . . at other characters, things: the intra-diegetic. This series possesses a certain reversibility: on the one hand, the camera looks, the spectator looks at what the camera looks at and thereby sees characters in the film looking; on the other, and equally, the spectator sees characters in the film looking, which is to look at the film, which is to find the camera's looking, its 'having looked' (the mode of presence in absence on which cinema is here founded). The first and second looks, moreover, are in a perpetual interchange of 'priority', of 'origination': the camera's look is found only by looking at the film but the former is the condition—one of the conditions—of the latter. The series of looks is then the basis in turn for a pattern of multiple relaying identifications (a term that would need to be carefully specified in each case): the turn between the first and second looks sets up the spectator's identification with the camera (rigorously constructed, with heavy constraints on, for example, camera movement); the look at the film is involved in identifying relations of the spectator to the photographic image and its movement, to the human figure presented in image, to the narrative which gives the sense of the flow of images, acts as guide-line; the looks of the characters allow for the establishment of the various 'point of view' identifications.

The power of such an apparatus is in the play it both proposes and controls: a certain mobility is given but followed out—relayed—as the possibility of a constant hold on the spectator, as the bind of a coherence of vision, of, exactly, *a vision*. Remember Bazin's fascination with the shot of Yvonne de Bray in Cocteau's (and Jean-Pierre Melville's)) *Les Enfants Terribles* (1950): 'the object of the shot is not what she is looking at, not even her look; it is *looking at her looking*'. The apparatus is the machinery for the fiction of such a position, for the totalising security of 'looking at looking'—and at 'her'. No surprise, therefore, that the achievement of that security, the institution of cinema in film, becomes the actual narrative of so many films, their relentless concern. Years after her single night of love, Lisa encounters Stefan once more at a performance of *The Magic Flute:* as Papageno sings 'A maiden or a woman' ('if a feminine mouth will kiss me, I'll soon be well again'), Stefan turns in his seat trying to seek out Lisa's face, the face of the woman who now—as always—is gone; an extreme close-up, pulling free in its extremeness from any simple assignation of a time and place in the diegesis, as much an index of the film's organizing activity, shows the seeking eyes, with Lisa commenting in her voice-over letter narration that 'somewhere out there were your eyes and I knew I couldn't escape them'; he follows her down into the foyer, 'I've seen you somewhere, I know'; and so it goes on, the entire film a problem of seeing and knowing, of the image glimpsed and lost and remembered—as of *the* woman, the mother (Lisa is always in Stefan's past, the time of his—and the film's—desire), the goddess ('the Greeks built a statue to a god they didn't know but hoped some day would come to them; mine happens to be a goddess').

Empire of the Senses produces and breaks the apparatus of look and identification; it does so by describing—in the geometrical acceptation of the word: by *marking out*—the problematic of that apparatus; hence its drama is not merely 'of vision' but, undercutting that classic narrative transposition, of the relations of cinema's vision and of the demonstration of the terms—including, above all, the woman—of those relations.

Throughout, the film is engaged with an organisation and movement of the intra-diegetic look. The very first shot after the credits is a tight close-up of Sada (Matsuda Eiko) lying down, eyes wide open, gazing off at the space 'in front of' the confines of the frame, at the camera, at the viewer-spectator; in the very last shot camera and spectator suddenly hold a position outside the character/space system previously established in this final scene and look down on Sada lying beside the dead Kichi (Fuji Tatsuya), her eyes open towards him, our eyes faced with the characters traced in red—in the blood of his severed genitals—on his body ('Sada, Kichi: together the two of us only'), while a voice-over, Oshima's voice, gives the news incident aftermath (Sada wanders Tokyo for four days, her case inspires a strange sympathy) and the date (this happened in 1936). Between the unresolved initial look from the screen, out of the image, and the abruptly found distance and voice of the close, it is the look that orders the sexual space of the film; with the narrative, as it were, the narrative of that ordering (and not of 'the incident'). From the start, the sexual is given in the image of the look (the assumption of the apparatus, thus of a film such as *Letter From An Unknown Woman)* but the look is then also given against the image, out of its 'truth', its mode of 'knowledge' (the apparatus discontinued, its coherence of a vision in pieces).

In the first shot, Sada gazes out; cut to a brief shot of another woman of the house who takes off outer clothing; cut back to Sada's gaze—from the opposite side of the 180 degree line, a peculiar and untied reversal of her position in frame—with the second woman beginning to caress her and, when Sada fails to respond, whispering 'you'll see'; cut to the two of them crossing an inner courtyard, snow falling, until they come to a room and crouch down to look in; cut not to what they see but to them seen seeing, to them seen from inside looking in, framed in the crack of the slightly opened partition, looking out at camera and spectator—a shot that occurs five times as they watch Kichi and his wife and that receives all the precedence of the scene. Thus, with a play on 'looking at looking', is set up a constant figure for the film: the sexual is seen and seen seeing; when Kichi and Sada make love, the look is passed elsewhere, to geishas, servants, always women.

This order of the look in the work of the film is neither the thematics of voyeurism (note already the displacement of the look's subject from men to women) nor the binding structure of a classic narrative disposition (where character look is an element at once of the form of content, the definition of the action in the movement of looks exchanged, and of the form of expression, the composition of the images and their arrangement together, their 'match'). Its register is not that of the 'out of frame', the *hors-champ* to be recaptured in the film by the spatially suturing process of 'folding over' of which field/reverse-field is the most obvious device, but that of the edging of every frame, of every shot, towards a *problem* of 'seeing' *for the spectator. 'Anata mo'* ('and you too . . .'): the closing words of *Death by Hanging (Koshikei,* 1968), themselves abruptly spoken in voice-over by Oshima, form equally the question of *Empire of the Senses*—where are *you* in this film and what is this film for you to be *there?* The earlier formulation in connection with the play on 'looking at looking' can be completed; the sexual is seen and seen seeing and the spectator seen in that seeing (there is a little précis of such a passage in the scene when Kichi and Sada make love in a Japanese garden while a woman nearby brushes the sand: as Sada sits down on Kichi the screen is filled entirely with the red of her kimono, over which image she comments 'someone is looking'); what is it to be the *viewer* of a film, to have its *view?* and with this film now?

The apparatus of look and identification is cinema's institution of a film's view and viewer (the point of that view), is the system of a film's *available* vision. Oshima's film finds the apparatus and its terms of vision as problem, as a specific construction (not a natural reproduction, a simple reflection), and does so exactly insofar as it poses radically—*absolutely* (an emphasis that will need to be taken up later)—the sexual in cinema and film. Inevitably characterised as the film in which 'everything can be seen', *Empire of the Senses* is acutely the film of the impossibility of 'the seen', haunted not by a space 'off' that must and can be unceasingly caught up into a unity, the position of a view for the viewer, but by a 'nothing seen' that drains the images of any full presence, of any adequate view: everything and nothing, the film is perpetually splitting, the division of the place of the spectator as subject in the troubling of sight and look. The most visible instances in the film (the paradox of 'the most visible' here is a version of the splitting, of the everything and nothing) are the shots outside the lovers' room on the two occasions on which one of them has just returned after an absence: the shots hold a partition wall (and in one case the empty corridor) through the thin material of which can be made out areas of colour and the human forms. No tease of erotic suspense: everything has been seen but there is something else to be seen, *nothing,* a more than seen, perhaps to be heard (Kichi's account of entering Sada: 'darkness ... seeing nothing... water flowing... blood, not blood, little red insects, in my eyes, nose, mouth... see nothing more... pleasure'), perhaps to be there as colour (the red that makes the surface of the film; colour is always potentially in excess of 'the seen', a threat to the 'objective' image and its clear subject). By contrast, it can be noted that the sole moments of the full image are precisely given as those of fantasy (a fantasy is an imaginary scenario in which a subject's desire is figured fulfilled)—Sada's picture of Kichi running on the hill as she sits in the train. Fantasy is the very régime of the image as totality, the inclusive coherence of the looked-for proffered as realised. Moreover, as Lacan remarks in a brief article on Benoît Jacquot's *L'Assassin Musicien (Nouvel Observateur* No. 594, 1976), 'fantasy founds the vraisemblable'; a film such as *Letter From An Unknown Woman* providing a sufficiently typical example of the foundation: the apparatus assumed as the establishment of a subject-vision (a vision of the subject) for the film which then thematically reflects and 'works over' in its narrative the terms of that fixed image-relation.

In Oshima's film, the splitting of 'the seen' turns on the development of a divided inclusion of the spectator. Thus the look out of the image already mentioned: a 'fourth look' which sends back and loosens the relay circuit of camera-viewer-character, the security of 'looking at looking'. Thus too the particular use of character look in the spatial organisation of the film, the construction of its scenes. Consider in this respect the 'wedding night': after the supper and the toasts, Kichi and Sada are encouraged by the geishas sitting round in front of them to consummate the 'marriage'; there begins a movement of cutting across the room between couple and geishas along the line of a look off into camera (Kichi's as he lies on top of Sada who this time experiences no pleasure, the geishas' as they watch), the movement continuing 'autonomously' when the geishas set up a separate action of their own involving a young geisha aroused by what she sees and whom they penetrate with a dildo in the form of a long-tailed bird. On the one hand, everything, a space filled sexually, both sides of the room held together for a toal scene, nothing not seen; on the other, that space broken in the very moment it is filled, the scene's total divided and the spectator's view given in that division, the repeated irruption of a nothing seen (and produced in the seen in the circulation and loss of the sexual and pleasure). The filmic figure of sexploitation is the pan, figure of the integral more, the *partouze* (the camera for the viewer *partout,* everywhere, an order of culminating plenitude); that of Oshima's film is this cutting as division, the summing of a space that always joins apart, elsewhere.

Empire of the Senses, moreover, has a scene in which the same figure operates, that has a structural and thematic equivalence to the opera encounter in *Letter From An Unknown Woman* (one of the points of ruinous remake). Fairly late on in the film, Kichi and Sada start to make love watched by an elderly geisha who admires their potency; Sada suggests that she would like Kichi; he touches the woman and moves on top of her to make love. The initial admiration-and-suggestion is shot from inside the lovers' room looking towards the geisha sitting in the doorway. Once the donation has been agreed, the scene pivots with a transition shot taken from one end of the corridor outside the room and showing Kichi squatting in the doorway to touch the old woman who is lying down facing away from the camera (Sada being off-screen, inside the room). The next shot completes a 180 degree turn, showing Sada in the room seen through the doorway from the corridor across the legs of Kichi and the geisha. The love-making is then given a series of some ten shots which cut between Sada and the geisha's face and between Sada and the interlaced bodies with Kichi looking round off into camera (at Sada; as in the 'wedding night' scene, on top of Sada, he looks off at the geishas); until the climax which cuts from and extreme close-up of Sada's lips to the old woman's face, eyes closed, false hair awry, to return to the angle and framing of the first shot of Sada from across the legs. The scene 'incompletes': from Stefan's image of the woman past, film's cinematic bind on the look, we are not held to an exchange—the two women, Kichi, and the absence, the other side—which terminates each image, the image, poses the problem, and the history, of the look in film, in cinema; the mother is dead (Kichi 'embracing my mother's corpse'), a flow of excrement, the looks fall off the screen, the film's space parts irreparably on the spectator; Stefan's seeking eyes, mirror for the spectator-viewer on whom film's narrative movement has been developed to insist, have been displaced as Sada's lips, the wound in the sequence, destroying the balance of the cutting on the look (itself already used to divide); Oshima talks of wanting 'to pass a shadow of death through the film' (interviewed by Ruth McCormick, *Cineaste, vol. VII* No. 4).

What is at stake in all this? What is being described here? With difficulty and uncertainty, it is a matter of trying to grasp in Oshima's film something of a real problematisation of the apparatus of cinema which engages immediately—indeed begins from—the various interlocking factors in the order that apparatus functions to obtain and maintain: image, look, their relation to the sexual. Bazin's 'looking at her looking' formula has been several times referred to; the same Bazin also talked, however, of cinema's potential for a 'quasi-obscenity of seeing'. The register of *Empire of the Senses* lies effectively *in the disphasure of look and sight:* the apparatus is pulled out of true, its guarantee of vision; the look divides and the spectator loses *the* view of the film, the simple position of viewer; a question then not of watching (watching is the mode of look and identification) but of what it is to *be seeing* the film. Such a question politically occupied Vertov, wishing to produce the disalignment of camera-eye and human-eye in order to displace the subject-eye of the social individual into an operational—transforming—relation to his or her reality; but it is decisive too, evident at least in the first five or ten minutes, in a film like Brakhage's *The Act of Seeing with One's*

Own Eyes (1971) with its pervasive pressure on invasion, the look invaded by seeing: show what cannot be watched at once in the shown (the morgue, the dissection, 'I couldn't look') and in the showing (the absence of any position of a look, the camera disjoined—in framing, height, movement—from the construction of a sense), remove—*dismember*—the coherence of a unified subject-vision.

It is not by chance that, after years of the history of the 'theatrical cinema' Vertov foresaw and loathed, the Brakhage film, like the Oshima, should be involved directly with death; the 'quasi-obscenity of seeing' is a profound connection of death and the sexual (the latter equally directly marked in *The Act of Seeing:* the fragmented bodies male and female). That connection is known in classic cinema but exactly as the violence and dispersion which apparatus and narrative are there to contain, and to contain on the image; the image, finally, of the woman: 'looking at her looking'. Think again of *Letter From An Unknown Woman* and its arresting gaze on the illuminated body of Lisa/Joan Fontaine, the film the theatre of that. The image for such a gaze is the centre and determination of the suspended scenario of narrative film, its constantly desired primal scene. With the apparatus securing its ground, the narrative plays, that is, on castration known and denied, a movement of difference and the symbolic, the object lost, and the conversion of that movement into the terms of a fixed memory, an invulnerable imaginary, the object—and with it the mastery, the unity of the subject—regained. Like fetishism, narrative film is the structure of a *memory-spectacle,* the perpetual story of a 'one time', a discovery perpetually remade with safe fictions.

This is the context of the particular economy of repetition in classic cinema where narrative is in fact the order of a *bearable* repetition. The coherence of any text depends on a sustained equilibrium of new informations, points of advance, and anaphoric recalls, ties that make fast, hold together. One part of the particularity of classic cinema is its exploitation of narrative in the interests of an extreme tendency towards coalescence, an economic tightness of totalisation; the film is gathered up in a whole series of ryhmes in which elements—of both 'form' and 'content'—are found, shifted, and turned back symmetrically, as in a mirror; the most simply obvious instances in *Letter From* include the café scenes (Stefan entering with Lisa to cancel a previous rendezvous/Lisa entering alone to look for Stefan), the train departures (Lisa bidding farewell to Stefan, her one night lover, for 'two weeks'/Lisa bidding farewell to Stefan, her son from that night, for 'two weeks'), the views from the staircase (as Stefan brings up first one of his many women-friends and then Lisa), and, of course, the carriage scenes which open and close the film, looping it round on itself. Engaged with narrative, deciding a narrative, *Empire of the Senses* has something of this patterning out: elements are given for narrative investment, to be related—used up—across the film (the knives that appear from the very first meeting of Kichi and Sada—'you should have something other than a knife in your hand'), rhymes are produced between scenes and scraps of scenes (the scene with the elderly geisha echoes and answers the scene earlier with the servant woman in the garden, just as it returns on the scene at the beginning with the old man who wants to but cannot make love to Sada). The notion of rhyme, however, already becomes rather uneasy, the possible examples lack the clarity—the evidence—of those that make up *Letter From*. In fact, what is in question is an economy that disperses the rhymes it half suggests into chains of elements—a shadow of death passing from the old man's unerect penis to Sada's face on the pillow next to that of her 'serious' town councillor, to the proprietor of the drink stall ('for a long time now it has only served me to urinate with'), to the black-shirted councillor again, to the elderly geisha, the maternal corpse—and brief starts of chains—from the bird-dildo inserted between the lips of the young geisha's sex to the mute old man who executes a bird-like dance, to Sada's lips pressed against Kichi's penis—that run on the surface of the film, freed from any articulation of 'form' and 'content' as a structure of obsession. Repetition in *Empire of the Senses* is consequently left as either abrupt or crude. The first mode is that of the organisation of the scenes in a succession in which they go repeating one another but without the derivation of any unifying memory from their succession, with no *narrative* pattern of recall, advance, resolution (hence, indicatively, the lack of transitional passages: a hand suddenly reaches out to seize a foot on the stairs or a carriage is suddenly seen crossing from left to right on the opposite bank of a river and a new scene is begun). The second, the final order of the film as it progresses, is that at work in the scenes of strangulation. Three times, and at length, Sada strangles Kichi; the repetition is crude in that each time brings no new information, brings only—precisely—death: the death finally of Kichi, and the fading of the subject, of the subject erect through a text, the given vision, the *direction* of and for meaning (thus the reaction of 'boredom': the loss of the narrative pact of purpose in time, of making sense, reaching a view).

Repetition is the return to the same in order to abolish the difficult time of desire and the resurgence in that very moment of inescapable difference. The edge of repetition—its horizon of abolition, the ultimate collapse of same and different—is then death; Freud can see repetition as the essence of drive and accord the death drives the fundamental place—beyond the pleasure principle—in his later accounts of psychical functioning. Relevantly for the present discussion, the implications of those accounts are brought out by Lacan in his '*Fonction et champ de la parole et du langage en psychanalyse*' (the essay translated by Antony Wilden in *The Language of the Self*, Baltimore, Johns Hopkins Press, 1968): desire is interminable, finds itself in a repetition that poses the limit of death as the 'absolutely own possibility' of the historically defined subject: 'a limit that is there at every instant in what that history has of completion; it represents the past under its real form; that is, not the physical past whose existence is gone, nor the epic past as rounded off in the work of memory, nor the historical past from which men and women derive the guarantee of their future, but the past which manifests itself overturned in repetition'; in short, 'the death drive expresses essentially the limit of the historical function of the subject'. *Empire of the Senses* comes near that limit of the subject, and, exactly, by repetition as loss of function, an absolute past to the subject forgotten in the subject-positions—with their own pasts (epic, historical, etc.)—erected thereon; but it can do so—a question in return to the frequent blindness of psychoanalysis—only historically, in the demonstration of a history, and a history of which here the institution of cinema is a part.

In its films, classic cinema is a certain balance of repetition: a movement of difference and the achievement in that movement of recurring images—for example, the woman as 'the same', a unity constantly refound. Narrativisation, the process of the production of the film as narrative, is the operation of the balance, tying up the multiple elements—the whole festival of potential affects, rhythms, intensities, times, difference—into a line of coherence (advance and recall), a finality for the repetition.

The realised narrative, the term of the process, is historically specific, is a mapping of the *novelistic* for the reproduction of which the cinematic institution is developed and exploited; the novelistic, that is, is the category of the specification of narrative in film, as in the novel to which cinema is made to furnish a successor. The title of the novelistic is *Family Romance* (or, a recent avatar, *Family Plot);* the problem it addresses is that of the definition of forms of individual meaning within the limits of existing social representations and their determining social relations, the provision and maintenance of fictions of the individual; the reality it encounters by remembering the history of the individual-subject. Narrative lays out—lays down as law—a memory in film from the novelistic as the re-imaging of the individual as subject, the very representation of identity as the coherence of a past safely negotiated and reappropriated—the past 'in' the film *(Letter From An Unknown Woman* with its overall theme of remembering within which a whole family romance can be carried along in fragmentary mnemic traces of a sexual history known and denied by its knowledge in these representations) and 'of' the film *(Letter From* with its direction, its rhymes, its constant images, its positioning of view for viewer, its unifying relations of the subject watching). Coming near to the limit of the historical function of the subject, *Empire of the Senses* is thus involved in and against the novelistic, in and against the cinematic institution as industry of the novelistic—which involvement is what the analysis of the film offered here has tried to suggest.

Kichi and Sada are the obsolete, the anachromism of the Okasaka section of Tokyo, the world of the geisha houses, the gay quarters. The film aims at the past which manifests itself turned over in repetition, its point is the sexual absolutely (as in the room, the closed world of the lovers able, says Oshima, 'to pursue their own pleasures'); but that 'absolutely' is historical, the limit of the historical function of the subject, of the institutions, cinema included, which serve to define the subject-function, and political, the social relations in which function, subject, institutions are in the last instance determined. It is the articulation of the sexual, the cinematic, and the political that, finally, makes the question of the film.

The political is insistent in the film, the punctuation of an outside, elsewhere to the room: children with flags—the *hinomaru,* the 'round sun', emblem of pre-war militarism—jabbing at an old man, the black-shirted councillor refusing to leave with Sada against a background of flying kites indicating the national Boys Day celebrations, soldiers marching through the streets watched by crowds of children again with flags, the voice-over at the end: 'this happened in 1936'; a crucial year in the growth of Japanese miltarism and the movement to military-dominated government, with an abortive putsch by a group of young officers in snow-covered Tokyo one night in Febraury during which a number of leading government figures were assassinated. The political is in the film, insistent in these punctuations, in brief echoes—the snow at the beginning, the room and Kichi's acount of being shut inside Sada (*Hakko Ichui,* the whole world under one roof, a nationalist slogan of the thirties)—but as the *outside,* the voice with the date is still abrupt at the end, a sudden distance back over the film, as though to state the necessity of an articulation between the sexual and the political and at the same time its impossibility, literally unthinkable.

Unless . . . unless one were to start from the very apparatuses of the establishment of the possible and thinkable, the apparatuses of representation and ideological formation, machines such as cinema itself. Hence the sexual, the political, *and* the cinematic. Hence *Empire of the Senses* as a film not 'about' Kichi and Sada, not 'about' 1936, but as a film working on a problem, towards an attempt to pose the relations of the sexual and the political in cinema, the sexual politics of film. The voice at the close is not that of the documenting of an historical past but that of the demonstration of a contemporary historical present; the question of a history that is *on* the subject *between* the sexual and the political, in that articulation and its encountered impossibilities; an encounter which is the condition of developing an understanding. To argue over difficult scenes (the rape of the middle-aged geisha, the egg), over the positive or negative aspects in the depiction of Sada, is in this context to miss the critical force of that encounter, which is a question not about this or that representation but about the fact of representation, the fact of representation in cinema. Remember perhaps that *Empire of the Senses* is not *simply* far from *Letter From An Unknown Woman.* What is the institution of cinema in film? the terms of its production of images? its operation of you, 'you too'? that *history?* The question Oshima.

March 1977

Reprinted with permission from Wide Angle *Vol. 2 No. 1 pp 48-57*

Postscript

'I look elsewhere and differently, there where there is no spectacle.' Hélène Cixous ('Entretien', *Revue des sciences humaines,* December 1977, p. 487)

Reading this article again at the distance of a year or more, it seems to me that its main failing, the result perhaps of the extreme closeness of the film at the time of writing, lies in a certain lack of directness in the way in which the question of *Empire of the Senses,* 'the question Oshima', is finally engaged. What is at stake thoughout, that is, is evidently (but with great difficulty) the whole problem of representation and sexual difference in cinema, the problem posed acutely by Oshima's film, this being its interest and its urgency (to stress which is to try to indicate something of its value for use, not at all to acclaim it as 'a good film', the latter notion precisely challenged by the question of this film to film, to cinema). Reactions, moreover, have been to that acuteness, the film equally rejected and assumed as important by feminists (for the assumption of importance see, as examples, the long review by Ruth McCormick in the issue of *Cineaste* mentioned in the article or the account given by Françoise Collin in *Les Cahiers du Grif,* October 1976), often becoming a point of reference by women (women not necessarily feminists) in those places where it has been commercially exhibited (this reference runs through the collection of testimonies and interviews edited by Marie-Françoise Hans and Gilles Lapouge as *Les femmes, la pornographie, l'érotisme,* Paris, Seuil, 1978).

Discussing *Letter From An Unknown Woman,* the article attempts to bring out in its analysis that the sole imaginary of that film is '*the* woman', the sole signifier the look as phallus, as order, as the very apparatus of the film—and of film produced as that cinema of relaying looks—which serves endlessly to remake the scene viewed, the theatre of the woman for the male gaze, the total spectacle. *Sole* imaginary, *sole* signifier? 'Sole' says merely that any difference is caught up in that structured disposition, that fixed relation in which the film is centred and held, to which the times and movements and excesses of its symbolic tissue and its narrative drama of vision are bound. The crucial issue in this context than becomes that of the place of women in that relation, the place of the look for women, an issue that has frequently been considered in terms of an emphasis on a lack of investment in the look by women; as Irigaray puts it: 'Investment in the look is not privileged in women as in men. More than the other senses, the eye objectifies and masters. It sets at a distance, maintains the distance. In our culture, the predominance of the look over smell, taste, touch, hearing has brought an impoverishment of bodily relations. It has contributed to disembodying sexuality. The moment the look dominates, the body loses in materiality. It is perceived above all externally and the sexual becomes much more a matter of organs that are highly circumscribed and separable from the site of their assembly in a living whole. The male sex becomes *the* sex because it is very visible, the erection is spectacular . . .' *(Les femmes, la pornographie, l'érotisme, p. 50).*

What the article seeks to demonstrate and specify as the question Oshima has its force here. *Empire of the Senses,* as the conclusion stresses, is not *simply* far from *Letter From An Unknown Woman,* is not outside the problematic of the Ophuls film, is rather its crisis discovered in a kind of radical proximity, pushing to limits, to limits of cinema and to the problem of representation and sexual difference in its field, in its very disposition. For a woman to take place in a film like *Letter From* is for her to represent male desire (to stand as the term of a social representing of desire determined by and redetermining a structure of division—the social operation of 'male'/'female', 'man'/'woman'—and oppression on the basis of that division—the difference assigned functioning as the inevitability, the right, of the domination of the one category by the other); equally, however, Oshima, in his own somewhat symptomatic fashion, says much the same thing of *Empire of the Senses:* 'When I write a script, I depict women, but when it comes to the filming, I end up centrally depicting men' (quoted in *Cahiers du cinéma* No. 285, February 1978, p. 72). Oshima's film does trouble, is effectively disturbing in the ways the article suggests, yet constantly rejoins *Letter From* on the very grounds of that trouble and disturbance—*cinema.* The question is finally that of the fact of cinema, of this late nineteenth-century machine (contemporary with psycho-analysis, itself perpetually worrying over what Freud calls 'the riddle of the nature of femininity') and its intrication in a specific representing function, a specific construction of a male desire (so too psycho-analysis? is the nature of those decisive encounters in its history—Breuer and Anna O, Freud and Dora, . . . Lacan and Aimée—quite by chance?). Yes, of course, the question is crude, simplistic (as is that parenthetically addressed to psycho-analysis), not allowing for the diversity of cinematic practices but remains nevertheless important, must inform any alternative practice, whether attempting to evict any scene and to grasp film in the process of its material effects (the 'structural/materialist' strategy) or to produce a different scene, a new relation for women (the 'new language' demanded by the Musidora group, for example, throughout their anthology *Paroles . . . elles tournent!,* Paris, des femmes, 1976), and this today above all when it is clear that images of women as woman's image have become a major focus of deliberate ideological concern in dominant cinema, from *Three Women* to *The Turning Point,* from *The Goodbye Girl* to *Coma,* in differing degrees of abjection. What the article wishes to stress in the movement of its analysis from *Letter From* to *Empire of the Senses* is that that is precisely again the question Oshima, the interest and urgency of his film.

Interest and urgency that can go beyond the particular context of cinema. Something of the terms of the article's account of Oshima's film are echoed, for example, in a passage in which Irigaray develops the idea of women's non-investment in the look: 'The possibility that a nothing seen, that a not-masterable-by-the-look, by specula(risa)tion, may have some reality would indeed be intolerable to man, since threatening his theory and practice of representation . . . '(*Speculum: de l'autre femme,* Paris, Minuit, 1974, p. 57). *Empire of the Senses* is crossed by that possibility of a nothing seen, which is its very trouble of representation, but that possibility is not posed, as it were, from some outside; on the contrary, it is produced as a contradiction within the given system of representation, the given machine. The problem is one of a specific institution of positions and relations of meaning, not one of an essence to be recovered, and the nothing seen is grasped as such from within that institution, as a point of and against its particular structure of repression, its particular construction (just as the 'invisibility' of the sex of the woman to which Irigaray refers is only a figure of an order that defines woman from man and sets her as the scene of his representation and power). Thus cinema divides not in any immediate sense on men and women but on these positions and relations of meaning of 'man' and 'woman' in its representations and its production of those representations, the subjectivity it engages; with the lack of investment in the look by women realized *there,* ideologically, not from something originally wanting in woman, women then being returned to a kind of archaic sensuality (a place in which they have been accommodated historically by men).

Occupied, even if in a provisional and limited way, with these issues of cinema, representation, sexual difference, the article is little occupied with *Letter From An Unknown Woman,* a film by Max Ophuls (is an interest in 'the work of Max Ophuls' today anything more than academic, the province of film studies and criticism? the question perhaps of the Edinburgh retrospective?). That 'Ophuls' is the name for a certain exasperation of the standard Hollywood production of his time is no doubt the case, as it is too that that exasperation is a veritable mannerism of vision, and of vision of the woman—with the masquerade become the very surface of the text, laid out, *exposed:* the masquerade of 'the woman' (the luxurious feminine of jewellery, furs, mirrors . . .), the masquerade of 'the woman in film', cinema's object, pursuit-and-goal (the ceaseless enunication of the ceaseless fascination of the ceaseless tracking of the woman for the gaze, the look, of her spectacle, of the desire to come there in a ceaseless momentum of appropriation which, in its extreme in *Madame de . . . ,* is near itself to the impossibility known, half-seen). A Hollywood film, an Ophuls film, *Letter From An Unknown Woman* is exemplary for the article, not typical, in its demonstration of the relations sustained in cinema, as cinema, of woman and look and narrative and scene, is itself, in that, not *simply* far from *Empire of the Senses.*
May 1978